UNFINISHED MASTERPIECE

UNFINISHED MASTERPIECE

The Harlem Renaissance Fiction of
Anita Scott Coleman

Edited by Laurie Champion and
Bruce A. Glasrud

Foreword by Cary D. Wintz

Texas Tech University Press

This book is typeset in Monotype Perpetua. The paper used in this book meets the minimum requirements of ANSI/NISO Z39.48-1992 (R1997). ∞

Designed by Barbara Werden

LIBRARY OF CONGRESS CATALOGING-IN-PUBLICATION DATA
Coleman, Anita Scott.
Unfinished masterpiece : the Harlem Renaissance fiction of Anita Scott Coleman / edited by Laurie Champion and Bruce A. Glasrud ; foreword by Cary D. Wintz.
p. cm.
Summary: "Collected short fiction of a Southwestern writer who published in The Crisis and other Harlem Renaissance journals. The stories offer commentary on the roles of women and African Americans in early twentieth-century America"
—Provided by publisher.
Includes bibliographical references (p.).
ISBN-13: 978-0-89672-629-1 (pbk. : alk. paper)
ISBN-10: 0-89672-629-0 (pbk. : alk. paper)
1. African American women—Fiction. I. Champion, Laurie. II. Glasrud, Bruce A. III. Title.
PS3505.O2774U54 2008
813'.52—dc22
2008000992

Printed in the United States of America
08 09 10 11 12 13 14 15 16 / 9 8 7 6 5 4 3 2 1

Texas Tech University Press | Box 41037 | Lubbock, Texas 79409-1037 USA
800.832.4042 | ttup@ttu.edu
www.ttup.ttu.edu

CONTENTS

Foreword: Why Anita Scott Coleman? vii

Preface xiii

Acknowledgments xv

Introduction: Anita Scott Coleman's Short Stories
and the Harlem Renaissance 3

The Stories

Phoebe and Peter Up North 17

Love's Power 25

Phoebe Goes to a Lecture 31

Billy Settles the Question 37

The Nettleby's New Years 43

Jack Arrives 52

El Tisico 59

"Rich Man, Poor Man—" 63

Pot Luck: A Story True to Life 72

The Hand That Fed 83

The Little Grey House   95

Three Dogs and a Rabbit   107

The Brat   118

Silk Stockings   130

Unfinished Masterpieces   142

"G'long, Old White Man's Gal . . ."   147

"White Folks's Nigger"   155

Cross Crossings Cautiously   162

The Eternal Quest   166

Two Old Women A-Shopping Go! A Story of Man,
Marriage and Poverty   170

———

Appendix: Arizona and New Mexico—The Land of Esperanza   177

References   185

FOREWORD

Why Anita Scott Coleman?

WHO WAS ANITA SCOTT COLEMAN, and why should we care about her work? From our perspective at the beginning of the twenty-first century, the discovery of an African American woman writer who published a batch of short stories, some essays, and two volumes of poetry does not seem particularly noteworthy. After all, we expect black women to write—indeed, we expect them to excel at writing. Literally dozens of African American women made their mark in literature in the second half of the twentieth century, and several have become literary giants. Maya Angelou achieved fame as a poet and for her autobiographical writing, Alice Walker received the Pulitzer Prize for her novel *The Color Purple,* and Toni Morrison became the first African American to win the Nobel Prize in Literature. And, of course, Zora Neale Hurston is honored as the pioneer who launched this tradition of great African American women writers. Today Hurston's novels and stories are part of the curriculum in literature classes across the country. How does a heretofore unknown woman from the American Southwest fit into this tradition? More specifically, how does

Coleman fit into this world of prize-winning black women writers, the most recent of whom appear regularly on *The Oprah Winfrey Show* to promote their newest bestsellers?

Given the fame and success of today's celebrated black women writers, it is hard to imagine that for much of the twentieth century the literary voices of black women were silent—or at least unheard. Zora Neale Hurston, acclaimed today as a star of the Harlem Renaissance, was dismissed by most contemporary critics—especially African American—and virtually unknown by all but a handful of scholars before she was "rediscovered" and extolled by Alice Walker. The Harlem Renaissance, long perceived as a male literary movement, actually gave us a significant body of work by African American women. Yet before the 1970s little attention was paid to the work of these women, and even today only Hurston and Nella Larsen achieve the attention they deserve. Meanwhile, outside of the literary centers of New York, and to a lesser degree Washington, dozens of African Americans wrote, published in local newspapers and small-circulation black magazines, and for the most part were ignored.

When I began my study of American history and literature as an undergraduate, very few literary works by African Americans were available, and studies of American literature rarely mentioned African American writers. My college text on the survey of American literature contained no work by an African American author—male or female—and it made no mention of the Harlem Renaissance. When I first began to work on the Harlem Renaissance in the late 1960s, only a few books of the writers of the period were in print, and it was very difficult to find the writings of African American women. One could locate a paperback reprint of one or two novels of Hurston or Larsen, but the works of other black women, especially poets like Helene Johnson or Anne Spencer or Georgia Douglas Johnson, were missing. The writings of these women, and many others, were resurrected in the 1980s and 1990s due to the persistence of black and women scholars who reassembled their work from countless newspapers, church publications, and magazines. Their inclusion deepened and enriched our understanding of the Harlem Renaissance, especially of the way it spread across the country and how it involved women. Today bookstores contain sections devoted to African American studies, and high school and college anthologies include Harlem Renaissance writers. Similar rediscovery projects have brought forth the works of Hispanic writers, black writers for other periods, and nineteenth-century women writers. Few of these rediscovered works became literary sensations, but collectively their presence redefined our understanding of American literature, history, and life, especially in terms of minorities and women. More important, these new voices gave us new insight into the experiences and the perceptions of minorities and women, as well as into regions of the country largely overlooked in the past. It is in this context that we must look at Anita Scott Coleman and her body of work.

Coleman was an especially prolific writer from a time, place, and caste that remain underrepresented in American literature. Her work records a voice mostly absent from American history. Born in Mexico, she spent most of her life in New Mexico and California during the first half of the twentieth century. Just in terms of time and place her work is significant. An African American woman's voice from New Mexico in the years shortly after its statehood is extremely valuable; likewise a new voice from California during the period of its black migration and its version of the New Negro Renaissance must be heard, and will add to our growing understanding of those movements.

As we examine Coleman's life and her body of work, we gain insight into a rarely examined class of the African American community. These literate, mostly middle-class black women from the 1920s through the 1940s worked and raised families, but also wrote and were published. Coleman was not unique. She was one of many who lived outside the cultural centers of America, but participated in the flowering of African American arts and literature during that time. Many women wrote poems and stories; many went unpublished. But some of these women did publish, discovering a great variety of outlets for their work ranging from national black magazines like *The Crisis* or *Opportunity,* to church magazines, local church bulletins or newsletters, local newspapers, or major black newspapers like Chicago's *Defender* or the *Pittsburgh Courier.* Those who published books either had them privately printed or had them printed and distributed through religious presses.

Coleman more or less followed this pattern. Her two books of poetry were privately printed, and all of her short stories were published in the black press. Most of these stories appeared in two lesser-known magazines that catered to the black middle class: *Half-Century Magazine,* published out of Chicago; and *Competitor,* a short-lived magazine edited in Pittsburgh. In addition she published in *The Messenger,* A. Philip Randolph's radical monthly magazine that focused on political and labor issues. Coleman surpassed many of her contemporaries by placing several stories in most notable Harlem Renaissance outlets—W. E. B. Du Bois's prestigious *The Crisis* and the National Urban League's *Opportunity.* This put her works briefly in the company of some of the best-known writers of the Harlem Renaissance. For the most part Coleman's literary efforts achieved much more modest results.

If Coleman were the only black woman writing in the Southwest at that time, her work would be important. However, she is one of several authors whose writings surfaced in recent years. Poet Bernice Love Wiggins of El Paso and California and novelist Lillian Bertha Horace of the Dallas–Fort Worth area are two other African American women writers whose work recently has been rediscovered and has or will be reprinted. The emergence of this group of writers and the potential that the work of others will emerge adds to the significance of Coleman and this collection of her work.

Finally it is through the rediscovery and the publication of works like Coleman's that knowledge and understanding of our past and of our culture can progress. Much the same way that the rediscovery of the mainstream African American writers of the early twentieth century brought the Harlem Renaissance to the forefront of American literary studies, and the rediscovery of Zora Neale Hurston and other women participants altered our understanding of both that movement and the role of African American women in American history and culture, the availability of the works of writers like Coleman has the potential to fuel new scholarship on the role of African American women in the West and their contributions to the art and culture of that region.

So, why Anita Scott Coleman? The answer is simple. It is not because she is another Zora Neale Hurston, but it is because she was an ordinary African American woman with not only the talent to write, but also with an extraordinary determination to do so. It is also because she lived and wrote and described life far away from Harlem and other centers of African American population, reminding us that the African American experience is not confined to Harlem or Chicago or the South, but that it touches all parts of America. It is because she rejected the path of other would-be black writers who followed the migration trail north or east to Harlem. Instead she wrote in the Southwest, and when she migrated she took the less-traveled path westward. It is through the work of Coleman and women like her that we gain a broader and deeper understanding of both American culture and African American culture, particularly the manifestations of that culture in the small towns and cities of the West, where a number of literate and educated black women put their thoughts on paper, and by doing so gave voice to the world they inhabited.

CARY D. WINTZ
Houston, 2008

PREFACE

ANITA SCOTT COLEMAN's fiction, essays, and poetry appeared frequently in prominent African American periodicals of the Harlem Renaissance and received prestigious awards, yet her work has since received little attention. Despite her geographical distance from the movement's intellectual and cultural center, some of her later stories remain polished examples of Harlem Renaissance literature. In the journals that published her, Coleman joined the ranks of such well-known Harlem Renaissance writers as Langston Hughes, but her development as a writer, ending with the lives of the journals themselves, seems sadly cut short.

A black woman born in Mexico, she was raised in New Mexico, where she resided when ten of her nineteen short stories were published. She then moved from New Mexico to California and published her final nine stories over an eight-year period between 1926 and 1933. In 1937, under the pseudonym Elizabeth Stapleton Stokes, she published a volume of poetry *Small Wisdom*. In 1948, another volume of poetry, *Reason for Singing*, appeared. The children's book *The Singing Bells* was published posthumously in 1961.

The themes and subjects of Coleman's writings parallel those of other Harlem Renaissance writers. Her stories provide commentaries on the status of black women, their role in black society, and the position of African Americans in an overwhelmingly white society. She emphasizes racial pride, the struggle of women for equality and independence, romantic relationships, and oppression owing to unequal distribution of wealth. She tackles key African American issues of the day, including white racist attitudes, gender roles, riots, passing, segregation, and unemployment.

General readers, enthusiasts of the Harlem Renaissance, supporters of black women writers, and students, teachers, and scholars interested in exploring Anita Scott Coleman's writings will find this collection invaluable. The stories are arranged chronologically to demonstrate Coleman's artistic development. Originally published as an essay, "Unfinished Masterpieces" is reprinted here as a short story because it exemplifies elements of fiction as much as it does the essay form. Indeed, "Unfinished Masterpieces" theoretically could have been published originally as either genre.

Although our introduction, "Anita Scott Coleman's Short Stories and the Harlem Renaissance," aims to encourage further examination of Coleman's work, this volume is neither a critical nor definitive edition but an act of recovery and preservation. So that this collection offers no distractions from the stories themselves, we have silently corrected obvious typographical errors. When characteristic of Coleman's peculiar style, unconventional spellings, punctuation, and word usage stand as originally published. Rather than assessing at what points in the writing, editing, or publishing process various anomalies both within and across the originally published stories may have originated, we have made silent corrections to reflect what we believe Coleman would have corrected if given the opportunity. The editors accept sole responsibility for all other errors and for any inaccurate judgments in the presentation of Coleman's stories in this collection.

LAURIE CHAMPION AND BRUCE A. GLASRUD
San Diego, California, and Seguin, Texas, 2008

ACKNOWLEDGMENTS

WE ARE GRATEFUL for the support from a number of institutions and individuals. Thanks to San Diego State University, especially Dean Stephen Roeder, for the assigned time Champion received to pursue this project. As always, the library staff at Sul Ross State University worked diligently to locate resources, including copies of journals, books, and periodicals. Thanks to Paul H. Carlson, professor of history at Texas Tech University and former general editor of the press's Double Mountain series, for encouraging our efforts. Thanks to two anonymous readers of the manuscript, who provided support and important suggestions, while also helping set the stage for this collection.

Judith Keeling, Texas Tech University Press editor in chief, has taken our project from manuscript to book; Keeling also suggested the title "Unfinished Masterpiece." Thanks, Judith. Thanks also to Karen Medlin, Erin McMurrough, and Lori Vermaas of Texas Tech University Press for their diligent work preparing the manuscript. Thanks to all the staff at the press for their encouragement and patience.

The short stories "Cross Crossings Cautiously" and

"The Eternal Quest" were originally published in *Opportunity: Journal of Negro Life,* published by the National Urban League, and are reprinted by permission of the National Urban League. The editors also wish to thank the Crisis Publishing Co., Inc., the publisher of the magazine of the National Association for the Advancement of Colored People, for the use of materials from *Crisis* magazine.

UNFINISHED MASTERPIECE

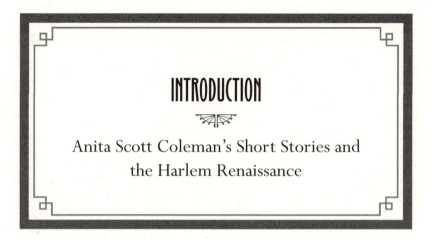

INTRODUCTION

Anita Scott Coleman's Short Stories and
the Harlem Renaissance

AN AFRICAN AMERICAN cultural reawakening known
as the Harlem Renaissance occurred on the East Coast
during the onset of World War I. Centered in the neighborhood of Harlem in New York City, the movement emphasized the political and cultural emergence of a "New
Negro." In general, Harlem Renaissance writers have received much scholarly attention. Yet, until recently, some
writers, particularly women, have remained if not ignored then certainly neglected. Anita Scott Coleman is
one of these writers. During the twenties and thirties,
she published award-winning short stories, essays, and
poems in national African American journals and magazines such as *Half-Century Magazine, Competitor, Crisis, Messenger,* and *Opportunity,* yet frequently she is excluded
from discussion of the Harlem Renaissance.

Also known as the New Negro Movement, the
Harlem Renaissance recognized the creative forces that
flourished in Harlem during the period between World
Wars I and II and stimulated black political, cultural, and
artistic expression in the United States. Never truly a
renaissance in the strictest sense, the movement contin-

ues to defy pigeonholing and to raise questions. Still, there seems to be a consensus. As Nellie Y. McKay notes, most critics "agree that *something* different from what had previously existed happened in black arts between the last years of the second decade [of the twentieth century] and the beginning of its fourth" (ix).

Although the Harlem Renaissance sparked an explosion in art, music, dance, and theater, it became synonymous with the literary output of the period. Renaissance writers of prominence include Arna Bontemps, Countee Cullen, Jessie Fauset, Nella Larsen, Langston Hughes, Gwendolyn B. Bennett, Zora Neale Hurston, Alain Locke, Claude McKay, and Wallace Thurman. Participants debated whether the primary focus of literary endeavors should emphasize achievements and accomplishments of African Americans, encourage stronger social acceptance of African Americans, or depict honestly and realistically the existing conditions of African American life. Writers such as Hughes, Hurston, and McKay espoused the latter course. Coleman also pursued this avenue in her portrayals of everyday lives and concerns of black Americans amid restrictive Jim Crow laws and racist and sexist attitudes. Despite differences in focus, all agreed the movement should celebrate African American heritage, inspire racial pride, commemorate African American culture, assume the rights of black citizens in a democracy, and fight segregation and discrimination.

Artistic and literary aspects of the Harlem Renaissance both clashed and intersected with African American political and social concerns of the time. Four prominent leaders vied for the support and manuscripts of the literati: W. E. B. Du Bois, head of the NAACP, published *Crisis* to support his goals; National Urban League editor Charles Johnson published *Opportunity*; the Universal Negro Improvement Association, a black nationalist group, and its leader, Marcus Garvey, published *Black World*; and Brotherhood of Sleeping Car Porters director A. Philip Randolph published *Messenger*. Each of these magazines and journals offered something seldom available in publications managed by whites: a venue for African American poets,

Reproduced by permission of the Crisis Publishing Co., Inc., from Crisis 31 (1926): 118

essayists, and short story writers, including Anita Scott Coleman, to showcase their work.

It is significant that many participants of the Harlem Renaissance were not native New Yorkers but migrants from the South and West who were drawn to New York City. To be part of this movement, others traveled internationally, including those who came from Latin America and the Caribbean. Prominent collector, bibliophile, and historian Arturo (Arthur) Schomburg came from Puerto Rico; author Claude McKay and historian J. A. Rogers from Jamaica. Caribbean writer and Renaissance author Eric Walrond was born in British Guiana. Coleman herself was of Mexican and Cuban heritage.

Not all notable African American artists joined the participants in New York City. Many contributors to this cultural rebirth remained in cities across the nation, including Boston, Chicago, Houston, Los Angeles, Philadelphia, and Washington, D.C. Among those who remained geographically distant from the center of the Renaissance was Anita Scott Coleman, who remained in New Mexico and California.

Born in Guaymas, Sonora, in 1890, Coleman was the daughter of a Cuban father who purchased her mother, a slave. He had fought for the Union during the Civil War and when it was over, he moved to Mexico and then the southwestern United States. Coleman grew up in New Mexico, matriculated at New Mexico Teachers College in Silver City, taught school, and later moved to Los Angeles. Her teaching career ended when she married. As she later remarked, perhaps revealing more than intended, "I did teach—long enough to consider it the most interesting work I've ever done. . . . And then I was married" (Murphy 36).

Coleman's ties to New Mexico specifically and to the West generally are most pronounced in her essay "Arizona and New Mexico—The Land of Esperanza," which appears in an appendix within this collection. This essay, in which she considers Arizona and New Mexico a unity and discusses opportunities the West offers both blacks and whites, depicts her fascination with her southwestern homeland. She discusses the landscape, including notes on the geography and geology, the wildlife, and farming. Into her detailed descriptions of Arizona and New Mexico she weaves insights into the role of African Americans, concluding,

[E]ver and ever the intrepid, stalwart Negro homeseeker forms a small yet valiant army in the land of esperanza.

And over it all the joyous freedom of the West. The unlimited resourcefulness the boundless space—that either bids them stay—or baffles with its vastness—until it sends them scuttling to the North, the South, the East whence-so-ever they have come.

For here prevails for every man be he white or black a hardier philosophy—and a bigger and better chance, that is not encountered elsewhere in these United States. (25)

After several years in New Mexico, Coleman lived in Los Angeles for quite some time. Although biographical details about her life are lacking, it has been established that beginning in the early twenties, she and her husband raised four children while residing in Los Angeles, where she managed a children's boarding house and continued her writing career.

As Quintard Taylor notes, "Los Angeles nurtured a fledgling western renaissance" during the twenties and thirties (245). In 1923, Arna Bontemps graduated from Pacific Union College and within a year left for the East Coast. Wallace Thurman enrolled at the University of Southern California and for a brief time edited the literary magazine *Outlet* to encourage a West Coast renaissance. While at USC, Thurman met Bontemps, who resided in Los Angeles and whose 1931 Depression-era novel, *God Sends Sunday,* was set in that city. Music and film were also important in the black cultural revival of Los Angeles.

By 1925, Thurman abandoned his efforts to establish a western "New Negro" movement and joined Bontemps and Langston Hughes in Harlem. Hughes, Bontemps, and other writers periodically visited Los Angeles's "ever enlarging artistic colony" (Taylor 245), where *Ink Slingers* and Fay Jackson's *Flash Magazine* continued the quest for a successful black literary journal in the West. In addition to publishing at least one piece in *Flash,* Coleman wrote scenarios for *Pathè* (*Crisis,* Jan. 1926, 118), the largest film company in the world during the early twentieth century. Coleman most likely was influenced also by visiting Harlem Renaissance authors. Certainly, her later writings point to an awareness of the movement's themes and styles.

All of Coleman's nineteen published short stories appeared in five magazines or journals—*Half-Century Magazine, Competitor, Crisis, Messenger,* and *Opportunity.* She began publishing short stories in 1919, the year she published four stories in *Half-Century Magazine.* The next year she published six stories, three in *Half-Century Magazine,* two in *Competitor,* and one in *Crisis.* In 1922, she published "The Little Grey House" in *Half-Century Magazine.* Her final nine stories, published between 1926 and 1933, represent the best of her fiction and have brought her the most recognition.

From the beginning, Coleman was in good company. Her stories ran alongside those of renowned writers such as Langston Hughes, Gwendolyn B. Bennett, Georgia Douglas Johnson, and James Weldon Johnson, whose *Autobiography of an Ex-Colored Man* was serialized in the same issues as her stories. Part of a sequence on the black experience across the United States, "Arizona and New Mexico—The Land of Esperanza" was serialized along with essays from prominent black authors such as Wallace Thurman, Alice Dunbar-Nelson, William Pickens, and E. Franklin Frazier. *Competitor*'s publisher was black newspaper magnate and attorney Robert Lee Vann, whose *Pittsburgh Courier* was the most widely circulated black newspaper in the nation by 1930.

During her short writing career, Coleman received several prestigious awards: "Three Dogs and a Rabbit" took the *Crisis* third prize for best short story in 1925, "Unfinished Masterpieces" won second place in *Crisis*'s 1926 contest, and her personal sketch "The Dark Horse," although unpublished, won second prize in the 1926 *Opportunity* literary contest. Coleman also received honorable mentions from *Crisis* for two other unpublished short stories, "Annie Hawkins" and "Flaming Fame."

Coleman's artistic development and reputation were encouraged by Wallace Thurman, who solicited manuscripts for *Messenger* in the mid-twenties. Abby Arthur Johnson and Ronald Maberry Johnson note Anita Scott Coleman among the "black writers with emerging reputations" who appeared in *Messenger* during that period (60). Her short stories "The Brat," "Silk Stockings," and "'G'long Old White Man's Gal . . .'" are the work of a more mature writer, one who has fulfilled the promise of "a writer of unusual ability," as she was hailed in a 1920 biographical sketch for *Competitor* ("Editors Note" 259).

Four decades after that accolade, Anita Scott Coleman died, her contribution to the Harlem Renaissance already forgotten. She wasn't the only black woman who for decades remained unacknowledged despite active roles during the Renaissance. The literary lives of women such as Georgia Douglas Johnson, Anne Spencer, Jessie Fauset, Gwendolyn B. Bennett, and Dorothy West met the same fate.

Neither white nor male, these writers sought to portray the place, role, and experience of African American women in a white- and male-dominated society. Only recently has the work of these women, and other black women writers, been resurrected by scholars.

As Alice Walker came to the rescue of Zora Neale Hurston's work, Ann Allen Shockley, in her 1988 *Afro-American Women Writers,* came to Coleman's. Reflecting on the marginality of black women writers of the Harlem Renaissance, Shockley notes that "the patronizing attitude of black male writers and critics toward black women writers forestalled their literary recognition" (405). Subsequently, Coleman's works have been represented in several anthologies, including Marcy Knopf's *The Sleeper Wakes: Harlem Renaissance Stories by Women,* Bruce A. Glasrud and Laurie Champion's *The African American West: A Century of Short Stories,* Venetria K. Patton and Maureen Honey's *Double-Take: A Revisionist Harlem Renaissance Anthology,* and Craig Gable's *Ebony Rising: Short Fiction of the Greater Harlem Renaissance Era.* Also, her works have been discussed recently in critical anthologies such as Champion's *American Women Writers, 1900–1945* and Lorraine Elena Roses and Ruth Elizabeth Randolph's *Harlem Renaissance and Beyond: Literary Biographies of 100 Black Women Writers, 1900–1945.* Mary Young's 1997 essay "Anita Scott Coleman: A Neglected Harlem Renaissance Writer," the first fully developed essay that examines her work, remains a seminal study.

Coleman's short stories reveal other topics and themes as well. Passing, for example, is significant in both "The Brat" and "Three Dogs and a Rabbit." In at least three of her stories, "The Hand That Fed," "'White Folks's Nigger,'" and "Cross Crossings Cautiously," white children are portrayed as caring for blacks, while their parents are outright racists. Family responsibilities and gender relationships are vital to "Phoebe and Peter Up North," "Love's Power," "Billy Settles the Question," "Jack Arrives," "The Little Grey House," and "'Rich Man, Poor Man—'." Race riots are central to "The Brat." Suggesting that whites don't always forget to reward blacks for kind acts, a character in "'G'long, Old White Man's Gal . . .'" notes, "now and then, white folks did remember the hand that fed" (82), a direct allusion to the title of one of Coleman's previous stories.

Even though she was from the Southwest, and later a resident of the West Coast, Coleman's earliest stories are set in the North and South, representing a North/South dichotomy rather than one representative of rural/urban or East/West. However, a few of her later stories as well as one of her essays focuses on the Southwest. In "The Little Grey House," Coleman points to home ownership and varied employment opportunities for African Americans in the Southwest. In a key episode of the framed narrative in "Three Dogs and a Rabbit," Coleman depicts an excursion to Texas. Her most pronounced story with a southwestern setting, "El Tisico" concerns issues such as immigration and blends Coleman's Afro-Latino heritage with her knowledge of the Southwest and Mexico.

In *Harlem's Glory,* Lorraine Elena Roses and Ruth Elizabeth Randolph point out subjects of women writers that capture the spirit of the Harlem Renaissance. These subjects include "the difficulty of establishing healthy human relationships . . . between blacks and whites" in a segregated society (7), the struggle to overcome rigid social limitations, the exploration of "personal identity amid contradictory definitions" such as African heritage (113), courageous fights against sexual exploitation, concerns about socially prescribed gender roles, extolling virtues and exposing warts of Harlem, and reflections of black women writers on their lives as women and as blacks.

Following suit, Coleman's fiction explores black identity, humanity, and love. It also stresses the role of family and community in black culture, points out economic disparities, and notes the emergence of an African American middle class. Although not to the extent of most other Harlem Renaissance writers, Coleman sometimes exposes racism as an oppressive social force. More often, she emphasizes the importance of the black family amid the struggle to survive financially, the roles women and men assume in romantic relationships, and the continual battle against African American stereotypes.

Whereas some of Coleman's stories allude to African American women's struggles for gender equality, they do not portray gender discrimination to be as repressive as it is in the fiction of Hurston, Larsen, and Fauset. But occasionally Coleman's protagonists do challenge social inequality directly. The trilogy "Phoebe and Peter Up North," "Phoebe Goes to a Lecture," and "The Nettleby's New Years" exemplifies social issues concerning the intersection of race, class, and gender. Independence is another cornerstone of the trilogy, and she encourages women to think for themselves, especially in "Phoebe Goes to a Lecture."

Most of Coleman's fiction reveals themes straightforwardly and relies heavily on plot machinations, such as twisted endings or framed narratives. For example, "The Nettleby's New Years" depicts its theme heavy-handedly. Phoebe Nettleby has planned an elaborate New Year's dinner but doesn't want to invite the Abbotts, who have recently moved from the South, because she views them as ill-mannered. A few days after Christmas, Pinkie Abbott nurses Phoebe's sick baby to health with home remedies, so Phoebe invites her family to the dinner, but Pinkie declines, explaining she wants a celebration for her own family. Phoebe buys gifts for the Abbotts, helps decorate their house, and buys groceries for a fine dinner so they are able to celebrate their Christmas on New Year's Day. Coleman openly announces the character's change of heart at the end: "How the next three days . . . revealed to Phoebe the happiness that comes with service" (15).

The framed narrative device is used in several stories, including "El Tisico," "The Brat," and "Three Dogs and a Rabbit." "Three Dogs and a Rabbit" employs this technique most complexly, revealing one framed narrative within another. The protagonist, Timothy Phillips, considers the elements of fiction such as plot, character, and subject matter. He then reveals a story he says effectively uses these elements, one he says will depict an inwardly beautiful woman. The story he tells, a framed narrative, involves a woman who protects a man running from whites who assume he is an escaped slave. When she testifies in court, she tells how she was beaten by her master for refusing to reveal the whereabouts of a hunted rabbit. She then exposes that she is the widow of a colonel, her former master's son. At the story's conclusion, Timothy exposes that he is the black man the woman referred to during the trial. "Three Dogs and a Rabbit" layers narratives to show how the narrators of each story reveal their hidden identities and to connect the enveloped tales to a unified theme.

Coleman's stories that depend on mechanical plot devices more often than not lead to didactic endings and might be best remembered more for historical value than for artistic appeal. However, several of her later stories reflect more innovative narrative techniques. For example, much more subtly than some of the stories mentioned above, "Cross Crossings Cautiously" depicts the plight of Sam Timons, a welder by trade unable to gain employment except as a handyman of sorts because he is black. While on a walk through town Timons crosses the railroad tracks, where he encounters the young white girl Claudia. Claudia asks him to accompany her to the circus because her parents are too busy. During the circus, Claudia's mother is delivered some type of a message and swoons, her father chases someone, and she is pampered the rest of the day. It's not clear whether her father kills the black man or merely chases him. In any case, at the end of the story, Claudia wonders what happened to the man who took her to the circus. Unlike "The Nettleby's New Years," "Cross Crossings Cautiously" invites several interpretations, while implying that it's sometimes dangerous to cross racial lines because whites might misconstrue kind deeds of blacks.

One well-crafted narrative device Coleman uses is second-person narration to talk directly to the reader, as in "Silk Stockings" and "Unfinished Masterpieces." "Silk Stockings" begins by directly addressing readers: "This is a plain tale of plain people. Have you ever thought about it," followed by a poetic explanation of the story, "In the most insensible or childish minds there is some train of reflection, which art can seldom lead or skill assist; but which will reveal itself, as great truths have done, by chance." The story then reverts back to addressing the reader: "Therefore . . . you have the gist of this story. . . . Unless you wish, you need not read on" (229). After this direct explanation, the narrator begins the story proper, concerning a woman who desires silk stockings, marries and has a baby, has a love affair, then rejects her lover when she sees a pair of baby stockings hanging on a clothesline alongside a man's rugged socks. Similarly, "Unfinished Masterpieces" begins: "There are days which stand out clearly like limpid pools beside the dusty road; when your thoughts, crystal clear as water, are pinioned in loveliness like star-points" (14). The story continues in the second person throughout, intertwined with brief passages of the narrator's memories of sculpting mud with a childhood friend. The story builds on the idea of shaping mud as an artistic endeavor to suggest people are God's unfinished masterpieces waiting to be shaped into artistic perfection.

"One of the best of the Negro writers," as a sidebar in the May 1928 issue of *Messenger* asserts (111), Coleman began publishing short stories in 1919 (often considered the beginning of the Harlem Renaissance) and published her final one a scant fourteen years later. One cannot help but wonder what else she might have done, had the journals who published her survived. Her all-too-brief writing career seems hardly finished and sadly underappreciated. Neglected despite her ability, published but overlooked, recognized but forgotten, she finally is beginning to receive her due.

THE STORIES

Phoebe and Peter
Up North

PHOEBE AND PETER had come with the first avalanche of eager wide-eyed Negroes to answer the call of the North.

Oh, isn't there something about people; who play the game fair; who take what comes and wrestle with it to victory or defeat that makes you long to grasp their hands and cry, "My brethren!" Phoebe and Peter played the game that way and this is just one little move they made on the checker board called life.

They landed in a big Northern city in September and before the first snow fell, Peter had launched full-fledged into the ways of the city. He dressed the part, acted the part, and very nearly overdid the part. But Phoebe still remembered the old home down South. She dressed the part of good, staid, a-way-down-South-colored matron. She acted the part and also almost overdid the part.

Peter used to say, "Honey, can't you fix your hair like the ladies do up here?"

And Phoebe used to answer: "I'm not going to stretch and pull and grease and burn out my hair, hear me, Pete?"

To which Peter used to respond patiently, "I can't say

how they do it, honey, but it looks mighty nice, their heads do."

Phoebe cried ever and ever so often, as often as Peter asked her about her hair. Tears you know cannot be hidden. It is real funny how they sag the cheeks, darken and inflate the nose, and make eyes weak and watery. Her tears weighted her down, consequently Phoebe didn't stay even as pretty as she was.

She did not look pretty to Peter when tired and hungry he came home from the foundry. Between the conflicting forces of fatigue, hunger and ugliness, Peter was a cross man. To think of seeing pretty women, thick as daisies in a field at every turn, until you get home, and there to find an ugly one. Why this would make a discordant note in heaven!

Peter began to delay his coming. He tried standing on the street corners or loitering in the parks, marking off the prettiest woman from among the merely pretty ones. That attracted him as an alluring game and you know it grows upon one like a taste for olives. So it made Peter a disciple. At times he skipped dinners and suppers and came home in the "wee small hours" of the morning, just in time for an early breakfast.

Phoebe quarreled and Peter quarreled, so they both quarreled. They quarreled and quarreled until Peter told Phoebe this:

"You can take a girl out of the country, but you can't take the country out of the girl, that's why you and I can't get on. You are chuck full of country. You won't dress and you won't look pretty. You are—you're—you're—" He searched his vocabulary for something fitting to say, then burst out with, "You are a thorn in my side, that's what you are." He slammed the door behind him to drown out Phoebe's sobs.

This happened in the morning and the noon hour found Peter still angry, so he spent his time down town with the boys and ate a solitary sandwich over a lunch counter. But during the afternoon, when nothing could be heard but the sizzle and buzz of machinery—which is silence to the foundry worker—his thoughts stole back to Phoebe. He remembered how pretty she had looked to him in another setting, in old Jenkin's cotton field where they had met, under the vivid blue of a Southern sky.

In memory, he saw again the fields of cotton, beautiful as newly fallen snow enhanced by glowing warmth and living green, and Phoebe's laughing face above it; her nimble fingers picking cotton faster than all the other hands; her skirts played with by the wind and showing her slender ankles; her strong young body poised erect despite its heavy load. He recalled how his blood boiled the first time he saw her in the field. It was then and there that he had vowed to take her from it and give her all the pretty things that women yearn for. Over and over he had repeated to himself, "I'll love her forever and forever," and now he had called her, his own dear little Phoebe, a "thorn in his side."

The hours dragged until quitting time. On his homeward way, he bought her candy at the first confectioner's, and fruit clustered prettily in a basket from a vender on the street. He paused once to look at some beautiful ermine in a window and felt in his pocket, sadly wishing it were pay-day. He hastened on, never stopping until he turned in at his own gate.

He pushed on the door; it was locked. This was something strange, he thought, as he fumbled in his pocket for his key. Finally, the door was opened and he was inside—but no Phoebe was there.

He placed the little packages carefully upon the table and looked about him, as he recalled, how back at home, Phoebe used to jump out at him with her face wreathed in smiles from behind doors and other hidden corners, but a moment's expectant wait told him that hoping for such now was useless.

He went into the next room and there found, spread on the table where his supper was invitingly laid, a note. It read:

Dear Peter:——I won't stay with you to be "a thorn in your side."
Good bye, Phoebe.

Peter dropped down disconsolately in a chair and buried his face in his hands. He smiled wanly as he went over the words of the note. How like Phoebe they were, his own, dear, high-spirited Phoebe, who wouldn't eat bread that she thought was given without welcome.

One, two, three days swept by, then a week, two weeks and still Phoebe did not return. Peter wandered the streets most of his spare time, only now, he was there for a purpose. Grimly he strode about, watching, watching, scanning every passing face with the hurt look of a collie in his straining eyes.

Then one evening when it would have been dusk, had not the city lights kept springing up one by one and in clusters, here and there and everywhere, in brilliant illumination, Peter glimpsed a woman— a blooming well-poised woman with very slender ankles. Her crowning glory was a head of hair. She was gone in the crowd, however, before the truth flushed over him that it was Phoebe—Phoebe—his own Phoebe.

Phoebe cried and cried after Peter left her; but his words were too stinging not to bring forth action. He had called her "countrified." She vowed that he should see. She gathered up some papers and searched their want ads for something that she might do. Like most gentle folk, Phoebe was a little wasp in action. Presently, she arose from her task and began to rummage in her wardrobe. She chose her most becoming dress, then remembering painfully about her hair, she sat down before her mirror, determined to do it up. She placed her hat carefully upon her head. When it was done, she caught up one of the papers and hurriedly slipped away a portion of it, putting it securely into her handbag and hurried out.

All the working force at the Bell-worth Hotel paused for a moment, as their manager strode past them, followed by a slender and somewhat doughtily clad, little colored woman, and disappeared with her behind the doors of Bell-worth's spacious pantries.

"Can't be the candy artist's helper?" was the question conveyed by each raised eyebrow.

Contrary it was so. Besides the art of picking cotton, Phoebe's tapering and nimble fingers could ply a needle deftly, but their real aptitude lay in molding, molding any plastic thing into any shape or form her fancy willed. She had made mud-dolls and mud-furniture, when a child; while her playmates had struggled with the intricacies of plain mud-pies. And once down South she had filled a white girl's place for a week, making sugar roses and frosting cakes. This was her meager store of knowledge. No object looms up so large that it cannot be overcome if we are determined to overcome it.

Monsieur Jacques Adonis watched the only one who had called in answer to his advertisement, for five minutes as she busied herself converting a shapeless lump of candy-syrup into a silver butterfly, before he spoke:

"You'll do: your pay starts at once; help me make these tulips for tonight."

Phoebe, an exulting Phoebe, stole into their apartment at five o'clock, one whole hour before Peter would come. She saw with dismay that he had not been in to dinner and then rebellion, born of independence, sprang to the surface. Though tired from her new employment, she flew about preparing something to eat for the man of her choice. While supper was cooking, she gathered a few belongings into a small valise, wrote the note and placed it where it could be found; and once more set out, this time to find a lodging place. In this she was successful, entirely so, because she found a room next door to Mayme.

Mayme Wilson was city through and through. Her coiffure showed it, her figure revealed it, her gait proclaimed it; and her speech was the essence of a city's slang. She was the most expert of all the hair-dressers at Jaynes and Hendricks Parlors.

Phoebe and Mayme became friends or as friendly as two so widely differing beings could be. It was the motive which causes a great big dog to stand motionless while he is being inspected by a very, very small one, that made Mayme kind to lonely little Phoebe.

And Phoebe worshipped Mayme because she was all the things from head to foot that Peter had found wanting in her. She meant, oh, how she meant to learn of this glorious creature.

Mayme had a way of throwing the weight of her body back upon one foot, then thrusting out the other in a manner to show off its pretty curved instep, and of placing her slim hands upon her slender hips, while dropping sweet crumbs of wisdom from her painted lips for the enlightenment of Phoebe.

No, kiddie, don't straighten your hair. It's already got the very wave that most of the old Janes around here would die for. Now, kitten, take it from me, be the wise Virgin, always do your hair low— that's your style. Listen, honey-bug, a man's loony, you've got to bluff him. You can't be easy. Don't wear your heart on your sleeve, hide it, keep him guessing, get me, hon?"

Thus it was that two weeks of nightly lecturings from Mayme and two months of pleasant lucrative employment found Phoebe a changed Phoebe. Her hair was worn in a way that Mayme could no longer scoff at. It would surely delight Peter. Her clothes had style and they were worn with a graciousness that was inborn.

In the meantime Peter had spent two dreary months. He no longer walked the streets but spent his evenings at home, in loneliness and bitterness. The thoughts: "Where could Phoebe be? What is Phoebe doing?" haunted him like bitter memories; pursued him like phantoms in the night and crushed him like terrible weights. It came dreadfully to him that wherever she was, whatever she was doing, he had driven her to it.

He imagined all sorts of dire things befalling his poor "countrified" (he still called her that), gentle, timid Phoebe. It took the taste for food from his mouth; and sleep away from his eyes; but he worked harder at the foundry and was promoted to a better position.

Phoebe's mirrors revealed the improvement in herself, but her heart yearned to have Peter see it also and tell her of it in his own picturesque way. She wanted him despite Mayme's "super-wise" advice.

"Don't you hunt him up. Don't you do it, let him find you. Take it from me don't be E-Z. That's a girl."

Such conversations were beginning to end lamely thus: "But oh, oh, oh, he'll never, never find me." Then a hasty shutting of a door and poor Phoebe would evolve out of her tearful state to find herself alone, no Mayme in sight.

It was one evening when she came in at five. It was one whole hour before Peter's quitting time, that she entered her lonely room, filled with genuine disgust. And how she did want Peter! She wanted to cook his supper, to prepare his favorite dishes. She thought of the little nut cakes he liked so much; she smiled in memory of the vast numbers he could demolish. Then, like a flash, came the conclusion that she was going home to make him some in reality.

Mayme from the next room called: "That you, honey? Come in here."

Phoebe answered, as she hurriedly stuffed some things into a bag: "Can't dear, I'm going home."

"*Home!*" A door flew inwards and a disgusted Mayme in a bright red kimono, stood framed therein saying stridently: "*You boob!*"

Phoebe was already out of hearing. Peter's lagging footsteps threatened to fail him altogether as he entered the hallway. His eyes flitted along the passage and he saw that his own door was a-jar. Could it— could it possibly be Phoebe; but who else could it be?

He ventured to enter and sure enough Phoebe—his Phoebe, a radiant Phoebe was there. There was a rapturous moment of laughter and tears and kisses all intermingled. Then Peter with masculinity asserting itself asked:

"Where have you been?"

Phoebe told everything she knew. Suddenly assimilating a well-known pose, with one foot back supporting the weight of her body, and with one foot front thrust out to show its prettily arching curve, with arms akimbo, with her hands on her slender hips; she quoted glibly stolen words from Mayme:

"And believe me, I'm the only lady of color on my job; the only one in my line. Why, Pete, I'm helper to the best candy artist in this old town—get me?"

But Peter being just a mere man could not see, he couldn't grasp the importance of Phoebe's employment. All he could sense was that his homing mate was about to fly, his drab, little housewife was spreading her wings. His male instinct cried out, "Beware," and a cold wave made a pathway of his spine; until some occult intuition, his guardian angel maybe, caused him to say these words:

"Listen, little girl, you can't work down there. We've enough money now to start on that little home you wanted, out in the suburbs."

Then not too sure of himself, he added:

"You used to want it, sweetheart, don't you yet?"

"Oh! Peter, dear Peter!" Then remembering Mayme's advice, not to carry her heart upon her sleeve, she stopped midway, poised herself with that lady's favorite pose—flung up her rounded chin and said:

"I'll be the only lady on my job. I'll have the homerule in my hands. Why, I'll be helper to the best old scout on earth, Mr. Peter Nettleby."

And with a hidden heart or not, Phoebe found herself cuddled closely in Peter's arms, his lips upon hers.

Half-Century Magazine 6 (Feb. 1919): 4, 10.

Love's Power

"BETH DEAR, I am in your Southland and yet—" Barbara burst out, then subsided into the aggravatingly interesting way she had.

Elizabeth, sweetly sedate with every Southern charm, from her soft, dark hair to her tiny aristocratic feet, echoed Barbara's "and yet—" as she lifted her eyes from a bit of fine sewing to look at her friend.

"And yet, I haven't seen any of that beautiful pathos or any trusting child-like spirit or any spontaneous joy-for-all feeling in your colored folks," concluded Barbara.

"Where is it? Where is it?" She screeched the last words in mock earnestness, fun gleaming from her frank blue eyes. This visit to the home of her college chum gave her her first glimpse of the South.

It was mid-afternoon. The sun blazed down upon the vine-covered veranda but a gentle breeze cooled his heated breath and the fragrance of honeysuckles and jasmine made that spot a pleasant nook for the two white-clad girls who sat sewing a little and chatting much.

Before replying, Elizabeth turned her eyes away from Barbara towards the sandy road, which stretched on and on, white and hot as far as her eyes could see through the green foliage. At the end of it she saw old Aunt Eppie trudging through the hot sand, her broad back patiently bent, one hand holding her skirts away from the powdery dust, the other clutching a huge bundle, which her arm could not surround. Elizabeth knew that her large, black, kindly face, shining with the sweat of toil, was spread with the quality that Barbara had called "spontaneous joy-for-all feeling."

Turning quickly to Barbara she cried, "Bravo! Here comes Aunt Eppie—"

"Goodness," exclaimed Barbara, "how can anyone stand all that dust in all this heat?"

"You couldn't and I wouldn't even try, Bobby," Elizabeth answered, "but Aunt Eppie does—and does it quite cheerfully. If she doesn't show us every one of her white teeth as she passes—it's my treat for the next candied fruit."

"That's it—just it," emphasized Barbara, "you have colored people playing a part in all your novels; you even manage to get it across in all your talk, as dispensers of brotherly love and about all most of them dispense is a wide grin. They are not kind to each other," she wound up emphatically.

"Oh you poor silly," declared Elizabeth before raising her voice in answer to the greeting from the gate.

"How's you-all today?" A quantity of sweetness rang in the Negro woman's voice—a quality that Barbara caught before Elizabeth had time to apprise her of it.

"I guess she fits into my joy-for-all corner," agreed the Northern girl, "and I feel cheered, friend Beth." Then Barbara sang in no particular tune:

> The week's wash's out,
> And the bacon and greens,
> Bubble high in the pot.

"I suppose that Aunt Eppie could keep a houseful exhausted with laughing at her drollness," continued Barbara.

"Up North, at home, there are lots of colored people—good citizens, most of them, nicely fixed, educated, and well to do, some are very rich, but they appear to be so very unkind to each other. They seem to delight and thrive upon the misfortunes of their neighbors. I think I have never heard of a real out-and-out, dyed-in-the-wool love affair among them in my life."

"That's because you do not know them very well," replied Elizabeth. "To me the characteristics you are searching for are sticking out all over them. Negroes are funny folks—I have known them all my life and yet I do not know them. They are open and free as the air, and still any one who has lived among them knows that they have depths that you and I can never plumb. For instance, would you see our cook as the heroine of a love story?"

"Stop it—stop it!" exclaimed Barbara hilariously. "That's a joke."

From somewhere indoors rang a soft, crooning voice; the sweetness and fervor marked it as unmistakably that of a Negro.

> On Jordan's rugged banks I stand,
> And cast a wishful eye
> To Canaan's fair and happy land,
> Where my possessions lie.

"Shoooooo—Barbara—she's coming; if she hears us discussing her she'll close up like a fish and you couldn't make her talk if you stuck pins in her."

The voice drew nearer, crooning more softly, ceasing as its owner appeared before the two girls on the veranda. She was short and rather stout. Her skin was that shade of brown peculiar to those whose ancestors have lived thousands of years 'neath a tropic sun; her hair, crispate and black, showed just a little bit beneath the frills of her clean white cap. Her large flexible mouth that seemed to be made for the sole purpose of smiling, revealed a row of pearly teeth. She carried a tray of tea things, fruit and sandwiches.

Barbara thought as she looked at her that if a genie could convert love into something eternally joyous and everlastingly care-free, then the glad-looking black woman before her might figure nicely into a love affair. But so long as love remained the soul-trying, meta-testing, heart-breaking thing it was, never could this happy woman before her have anything in common with the little Love god.

"Annie," Elizabeth was saying in a voice that Barbara had never heard before, "put the tray on that small table. How is Ben today?"

"Oh, he is not so well, Miss 'Lizabeth. He didn't sleep one bit last night—not one single wink; that's honest."

"That is too bad," replied the Southern girl, still using the new tone of voice. "And who?—surely Ole Mammy did not have to stay up with him all night?"

"Indeed she didn't. I did that myself," said Annie as she stopped arranging the fruit in the basket, turning to face her mistress proudly. "What you 'spose I married Ben for, Miss 'Lizabeth?"

The Northern girl knew she was forgotten, at least by the little, fat, dumpy colored cook. The semi-shy, semi-sullen manner invari-ably worn in her presence had fallen away. Barbara was amazed at the strange beauty, or was it pathos—shining in the girl's black face, as she reiterated, "What you 'spose I married him for, Miss 'Lizabeth?"

"To work for him is about all, I think, Annie. That is all you do—work here all day and nurse him all night."

"Yes'm."

Barbara marveled at the light in her eyes—the glowing un-quenchable fires of the great bruised heart of a fun-loving race.

"Yes'm, that's all as you can see. But I don't regret it. I—I wouldn't swap my life for yours, no'm, not for worlds. I have Ben, Miss 'Lizabeth," she added naively. "During the day, in your kitchen the water gets to boiling in the kettle and it sings to me, 'Ben loves you,' or maybe it being teasy, sings, 'Go on child, you love Ben.'

And the churn—I like to make butter, just so I can hear it going, 'He loves—you love—he loves.'"

"At night of course it's hard on Ben, Miss 'Lizabeth. He isn't used to the pains in his body yet and he is not used to lying flat on his back all the time. But you ought to see how that man's eyes can shine when I open the door and pops my head into his room. You ought to hear his voice cuddling down to honey-tones just for me."

Annie paused, her black face all aglow, her soft eyes softer yet, gazing into space, seeing beautiful visions above the toil and pain which bound her.

"What does the doctor say?" inquired Elizabeth, gently.

"Oh, he says Ben is most all right, only his back will always be out of fix, but he is going to be able to sit in a wheel chair; then I can move him about—that's something, Miss 'Lizabeth, to always have your man where you can find him."

Her big mouth flashed open in its wide smile. Though now, Barbara saw not the display of pearly teeth but the indomitable spirit that could bravely smile through tears. With a deft movement she whisked the tray from the table and disappeared through the open door.

To Canaan's fair and happy land
Where my possessions lie.

The voice rose and fell plaintively as it wafted back to the silent girls.

"Bobby, did you understand it at all?" questioned Elizabeth, softly.

"Yes, yes," answered the Northern girl, "how did such a thing happen?"

"It's a simple story. Annie has been married three years already. Two weeks before her wedding, Ben was hurt, mangled out of all semblance to his former self, in a train wreck. He carried a small insurance and was buying a little home—the one in which they live—on the installment plan, when the dreadful thing happened. He was all the support his aged mother had, so you can see how things stood. Nevertheless, Annie married him, to take care of him and his old mother. She is still on the job, Bobby, true blue—tried and true, if ever a human can be.

"The doctor tells her he will be able to sit in a chair some day, but even that small joy is not to be. All of us know it except her. Dr. Martin told me that with the care, the positively luxurious self-sacrificing attention she gives him, he will drag on, a helpless wreck—none can say how long.

"It's their love for each other that keeps the spark of life burning in his battered body. He suffers dreadfully, poor fellow."

"I wonder," cried Barbara earnestly, "could I do as much for mine—and not complain?"

"Would I for mine?" questioned Elizabeth.

Half-Century Magazine 6 (May 1919): 6.

Phoebe Goes to a Lecture

"I TELL YOU, kitten, you come with me next Friday," said Mayme to little Phoebe, as they sat together in the latter's cozy sitting-room.

"Get this straight, hon, you're staying too close. It's the ticket maybe, to always stay to-home and run your household ship-shape—but take it from me, kid, it's killing. I would not do it. Why, hon, a gold man couldn't take all my joy out o' life. Now, listen to me, doll-up your prettiest Friday and come into town. I'll be at Donald's sharp at two for ices you know, then we will beat it to the Wise-Acre Women's Club-rooms. There's going to be a lecture and I'm the appointed queen, kid, who has to attend to boost up trade for Jaynes and Hendricks Beauty Parlors. All I have to do is slip 'em over some especially printed cards—some swell they are too—we figure on getting some mighty paying trade. All you got to do is once get your intellectual doll-babies headed for beauty, kid, and they make a home-run every time."

"Say it is a go?" she wound up a bit breathlessly to gaze scrutinizingly at Phoebe.

Phoebe sat listlessly beside the open window, the sewing in her lap forgotten.

"Why yes, I suppose so," she agreed as she turned to face her friend somewhat languidly. "Peter was saying this morning, that he thought I should go out more, but oh, dear," she sighed, "this place is so large, Mayme, and I do not know the people and most of them I meet are so distant and unfriendly. I'd rather stay at home. You see I love my flowers and my books, and haven't you noticed, I am collecting copies of famous paintings, it's such fun to get them and read up on the lives of their painters."

Mayme's assent to this was a dismal "grunt," then she added: "I think you've a twinge of homesickness, honey-bug, but you'll outgrow it. Magnolia blossoms and sunny weather are pow'ful fine, I'll admit, but I'll take the North and snippy-snappy city life for mine—see? Gee-ee, I'm overstaying my time." As she spoke, she was up, and rapidly gathering her belongings, prepared to go. She darted towards Phoebe impulsively, pecked a kiss upon her cheek and patted her shoulder affectionately: "You are down in the dumps, kitten, but meet me Friday. That's a girl." And so saying she hurried away.

"I declare," murmured Phoebe, "Mayme is a real tonic—what would I do in this lonesome place without her?" Then wonderingly she thought: "Dear old Peter, what would he do, if he really knew how dreadfully homesick I am. It's a shame, too," she thought contritely, "everything here is so different, so uplifting, it's inspiring just to be here, and down home," she pressed her lips tightly; as she thought pityingly of the friends—"down home"—

"I am a goose," she said the words aloud uttering them vehemently—wholly absorbed with her thoughts.

"TUT-TUT, I don't think so," returned Peter. He stood in the door-way regarding her roguishly.

Phoebe, startled, sprang from her seat, then laughing ran to him flinging her arms about his neck.

"How on earth did you get in without me hearing you?"

"Easy enough while you were busy calling yourself names," retorted Peter. "How long have you known you were a goose and how does it feel?" he teased.

"That's my secret," rejoined Phoebe. "Guess who's been here?"

"The Mayor's wife," responded Peter in mock surprise.

"Guess again."

"Nixy," laughed Peter, "I met Mayme on the corner—gave me a raking over about you, said I ought to see that you got a little diversion—bet me a dollar to a doughnut I'd find you crying right where she had left you—that's why I slipped in—the old girl owes me a dollar—I'll make her pony up too," he declared, relishing the outcome of their good-natured wager.

"But see here, little girl, aren't you happy?" His gay manner changed instantly to one of honest concern; as he drew Phoebe into his arms and turned her face to his, that he might search her eyes.

"Why, of course, I am, Peter—but—," Phoebe's mouth trembled perceptibly. "I *am* a goose, Peter, just as I said a while ago because there are times that I can't help thinking about our old home. I seem to smell the flowers and I see old Aunt Susan and Uncle Alex and all the youngsters. Why, I even miss the cotton-fields and I seem to ache for the warmth and friendship that we left behind us. I long for the smiles and the 'howdies' that everyone used to give me as I passed along the street—and here—oh, Peter, everything is so strange and so unfriendly."

Peter's arms tightened about her, for he too had felt, but kept hidden, the mighty tugging of his heartstrings for the old home and the old environments so full of good-humored friendliness; which all the limitations and restrictions put on his race could not smother. It was there, say what you would, the open hand and the open heart of friendship, a blessed thing, grown luxuriant among his oppressed people, back there in the sunny Southland.

"You can forget it all in time, sweetheart, only," he added soberly, "we don't want to forget, do we, little girl? We are going to hold on to our pleasant memories as we would to sacred things, but there are unpleasant memories too—hateful ones, Phoebe, and they are the ones that are going to make us hold on here and keep us here. No! We must never forget, neither the good or the bad, for together, they are the chains that bind us to the path we are started on. We've got to live and make a way for others—the little ones—our little ones maybe, and down there, girl, we can't even have the chance."

Phoebe's arms were flung upward now to encircle Peter's neck; as solemnly they stood oppressed by the weight of color; but dauntless, determined to surmount it.

Friday came. It was a clear day, warm and sunny. The scent of budding things and the fragrance of newly upturned earth was everywhere, for in the city, little plots of ground were already spaded up for planting—thanks to the high cost of living.

Phoebe inhaled the balmy air joyously as she went along Broad Street. It was almost two, and she knew Mayme was even then waiting for her at Donald's. "Dear, kind Mayme, is always as punctual as the old clock, in the city-hall back home," thought Phoebe happily.

"Oh, you doll," sang Mayme gaily as Phoebe entered Donald's exquisitely appointed ice-cream parlor. Donald himself, the brown and dapper little proprietor, ushered her to Mayme's table.

"I second the motion," put in Gordon Moss, rising from a seat beside Mayme to greet Phoebe cordially, while Roscoe Donald's eyes implied that he thought the same.

"Oh, Gordon," exclaimed Phoebe delightedly. "Mayme didn't say you would be here too."

"Why, his real name is Goatee Buttinsky," drawled Mayme. "Can anyone tell just when a goat decides to butt? Oh, no," she answered her own query drolly. "You never know until he has landed the butt."

"If that's the way you feel," replied Gordon dolefully, "I'll leave." He began to rise but was restrained by a deft move on the part of Mayme.

"Oh, no you don't, not on your life. You talk to that waiter!" she ordered threatenly.

Gordon laughed and settled himself comfortably in his chair, pleased as he always was, to be commanded by the sparkling, audacious Mayme.

Half an hour later Phoebe and Mayme were on their way to the Wise-Acre Women's Club. The lecture hall was spacious and Phoebe found herself in a maze of women—big ones, chubby, fat, and slender ones, women manicured and tailored, business-like and militant, bespectacled and lofty-browed; but in all that throng of women, Phoebe herself was the only woman there belonging to the time-honored school of home-loving wives.

Now and then, she caught glimpses of Mayme in her place near the entrance standing there so alert, so busy, distributing the little cards, one after another to the ever gathering horde of women.

Presently an exceedingly aggressive looking spinster mounted the platform, and instantly the buzzing of many subdued voices ceased; as if by magic, there was quiet.

The lady before them was Doctor Patty Hugh, the foremost and most accurate authority on birth-control known.

Ah, and she could talk. Her sonorous voice made itself heard, and felt, in every corner of the vast room; and besides she was such an ardent devotee to the science she was eulogizing.

Phoebe felt that it was indeed a heinous crime to be a mother. Also, she thought by the determined quirk that sat upon more than one mouth, that few indeed would be guilty of the grave offense among those present.

She wished she had not come. Was this the sort of lectures women attended? How different to her old home training, wherein maternity had been upheld as woman's crowning glory, and little ones as the Lord's anointed.

She was glad when she was outside. Glad indeed, when Mayme threaded her way painstakingly to her side and cleverly maneuvered a way out of the crowd and into a quiet side-street, where they could walk along leisurely.

Mayme watched her amusedly, finally asking, "How'd you like the spiel, kitten?"

"Gracious, it was horrid," blurted Phoebe earnestly.

"D'ye think so? Oh, well, it's good food for thought. You've got to go some to refute all that old lady-quack's arguments, now don't you? Own up."

"Yes," faltered Phoebe.

"All right then," exclaimed Mayme. "Honey-child, that's why I urged you to come, not that I thought you'd enjoy that especially, but get out, see with your own eyes and hear with your own ears, and give your brains an airing. That's what city life is for, to put the 'pep' in living. You don't need to think other people's thoughts. Think up your own; but you can't think looking inside yourself. You've got to look out. Do you get me? Then you won't have time for such nonsense as loneliness."

"What a dear, dear friend you are," cried Phoebe.

They had stopped at their place of parting while a jitney drove up to the curb.

"Bye-bye," chirped Mayme gaily and her sparkling eyes beamed lovingly upon Phoebe an instant before the door of the car swung shut.

"Good-bye," said Phoebe, and then, quite contentedly snuggled back among the cushions to gaze out upon the broad smooth road; which led to home and Peter.

Half-Century Magazine 6 (June 1919): 6.

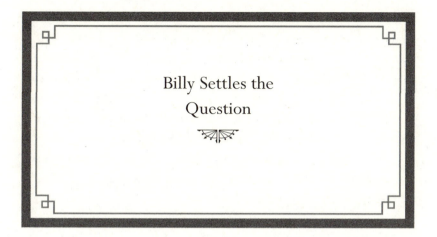

Billy Settles the
Question

THIS STORY would be just another of the many triangles if it were not for Billy. The young Reverend Duncan, since he plays the smallest and yet the greatest part in this story, needs no lengthy introduction. That he was in that class of men into which women rush blindly in search of husbands, is proven by the mere statement that both Martha and Miss Upton were—to put it bluntly—in pursuit of him. As a husband—let's see, being a parson, he would thereby be a poor provider; being a very smug man, he would never be indulgent; but, being slow, and for the most part bent toward righteousness, he would, perhaps, be faithful—at least the women gambled on that.

Martha was Martha. That is a simple way of saying that the vampire lady in this tale was a *stunner.* To hear her, say twice, you remembered her always. When she passed along the street, people spun around to take a second look—to stare. She was so healthy, so glowing, so vibrant and so plump. Her hair was sandy with ripples in it, shining like burnished copper, and her eyes, big and black, sparkled like twin pools in the sunshine. She dressed cleverly, and as she walked she clicked the heels of her dainty boots resoundingly against the pavements; some would say to attract attention. She had passed the garden of her youth and for several years had lived in the wide acreage of womanhood. Ah, Martha was no inexperienced maiden. She had tasted of all the cups which hold the different broths of life. In the past she had been wedded, and her child, the child of that union, was the one and only cup from which she had tasted, whose contents she was willing to drink to its dregs. Little Billy was Martha's heart. In him could be found the only invulnerable spot in the crust like armor; which a rugged life had given her.

She was intensely interested in Reverend Duncan for, well—several reasons—for one thing, she was tired. It is a difficult task, to lure, say, a half a dozen beaux to a given position to stand incessant barrage, and keel them from retreat, or, worse yet, an advancement. She was bored with her nomadic existence. Martha lived in a town only so long as her beaux proved useful and untroublesome. But the main reason for her attack upon the parson lay in Billy. The little shaver was growing up and to use Martha's own expression, "he needed a daddy." Already she had captivated the Reverend and she did not intend to let up until she had the noose of matrimony securely about his neck. So much for Martha.

To her parents, the able and well-to-do Luther Uptons, Miss Nina was a goddess of beauty. To the pupils of the third grade, class B, Lincoln Center School, she was also a fairy creature decked in beautiful garments. But to others who looked upon her with the critical eyes of the unloving, Nina Upton was only a very slender little brown-skinned lady with a tilted nose and pretty black eyes. You could have brushed past her twenty times on your way to town as she threaded her way to school, and unless she dropped her notebook or a pencil at your feet, her proximity to you would go unnoticed. Truly, Miss Nina was a demure, inexperienced maiden; she, as yet, had sipped from no cup of life save that of loving-kindness. She was as tender as Martha was rugged, as simple and true as Martha was wise and shrewd. She had none of the dazzling qualities of which Martha had a triple share. You had first to learn the winsome sweetness of Miss Nina, before you became aware of the soft warmness of her eyes, and the pleasant good-natured quirk on her lip, and the taste for fun that lurked in the tilt of her nose.

She had come to love Reverend Duncan while sitting on Sunday mornings under the sound of his voice. The Reverend's voice was admirable and he was an adept at giving a musical swing to his most tiresome sermons. Then, too, she saw him while teaching in his Sabbath School and while singing in his choir. During the week they often met for quiet conferences pertaining to their mutual work. In fact, so frequent and so pleasant had been these little tête-à-tête conferences that the Reverend Duncan had learned to look with satisfaction into Miss Nina's bright eyes; many times he had laughed uproariously at her quaint, gentle humor and—I must tell it—he had kissed the pleasant quirk which played so kindly on Miss Nina's lips.

Even Nina's parents had begun to consider the Reverend's visits as forerunners to the inevitable question. It mattered not that old man Upton regarded him as a pig head, a goat head and a block head; he didn't care a fig for no man paying court to his daughter, "*doggone 'em!* His little girl was too good for 'em." But Mother Upton encouraged the Reverend and in discreet moments, called him son, with meaning inflections in her voice. He was her pastor, bless you, and soon to be her son, she hoped, so the kind old soul baked huge, mellow, yellow meated cakes and set them apart for his coming.

Things were as bright as newly scoured tin pans, seemingly no cloud lay on the bright horizon of Nina's life. Love and youth were hers and she was happy, as sweet as a sprig of honeysuckle and as gay as a scarlet poppy . . . then Martha intruded.

There is no need to go into details of how she made her first move of intrusion. Sufficient to say that she intruded, with all her manifold charms mustered as for war.

Martha could sing, too. That was known as soon as she made her appearance in the choir one Sunday morning. Young Reverend Duncan was justly proud of his discovery as he listened with every one else, to her deep-throated contralto spreading over the church, out through the windows to die in echoes against the opposite buildings, sweet, unrestrained and powerful. Why, it quite drowned out the voices of the other singers, especially Nina Upton's plaintive soprano.

And it followed that the Reverend gentleman began to take himself to Martha's home, to talk of things pertaining to the choir, of course. Only, several luscious cakes Mother Upton baked grew stale and some of the warm lights died in Nina's eyes and the pleasant quirk became a pathetic droop on her lips.

Now, Billy, Martha's little Billy, was a pupil in the third grade, class B, Lincoln Center School, and as you know, Miss Upton was the teacher. Billy had long since fallen under the spell of the few though enduring charms which Miss Nina possessed. Why, he even adored the sound of Miss Nina's voice and he reached the very acme of bliss on those occasions when Miss Nina squeezed herself down into the seat beside him, and bending her head very near his own, helped him with his figures. Billy couldn't see how one dumb figure like "0" could borrow from "8," its side-partner, to lend in turn to "9," the digit who lived downstairs. But it was a joy to watch him, the sturdy little man-child trying to grasp any and all the problems which unfolded themselves for a third-grader, class B, under the guidance of a wonderful Miss Nina.

Some masculine intuition, perhaps, kept Billy from confiding in his mother. He had never told Martha what a chunk of his heart had gone to Miss Nina. Poor little chap, he divined even at his tender age, the jealousy of woman.

Things, to be sure, would have swung right on, with Nina breaking her heart while Martha circled the marriage noose nearer and nearer the minister's head, had not little Billy become very ill, very very ill, his little body throbbed and ached and writhed in pain, and he lay and moaned as only the child sufferer can.

Forgotten, in Martha's mind was the Reverend; swept from her memory a half a dozen other beaux; ignored, the latest cut and the nobbiest fashion in clothes; disdained, uncombed, all the wonderful sandy hair; kicked aside were the high-heeled boots, that could be made to click so takingly. Now, her feet clad in thin-soles, rubber heels, flew here and there about a darkened room, and carried her often, oh, so often, to bend over a little bed, where a tiny, pain-racked youngster lay.

Over and over came moans from the parched lips. Suddenly the doctor drew away from his little patient to say quietly over his shoulder, "Martha, the little tad is saying something—listen."

Over and over came the moaning voice, now louder, now beseechingly. They listened together—the doctor, the minister and Martha. Over and over, again and again it was repeated, while Martha, hardened and relentless, yet mother, stooped nearer and nearer, striving to catch their meaning. A pitiful Martha finally jerked herself erect. Her eyes were wide and hurt, while in dry, breathless tones she interpreted her little boy's moans. "He-is-saying-his-teacher's-name—Miss Nina—Miss Nina. . . ."

"Miss Nina? Now who? . . ." questioned the doctor, stopping short before the look of painful misgiving on the faces of the minister and Martha. "Well," continued he, "his fever breaks one way or the other in an hour. Whoever this Miss Nina is, get her here, if possible, for the critical moment. Her presence may have the power to pull him through, though my medicines fail."

The young minister discreetly lowered his eyes; he hoped most heartily that Martha would not send him for Nina. Lifting his eyes furtively he saw with relief, that Martha had already thrown a scarf over her head—already her hand had turned the door-knob. She threw a lingering glance towards the bed, unseeingly her eyes passed him and she was gone.

A half hour later Martha returned with Nina. Unhesitatingly, Nina went to the bed and, bending over it, laid her gentle hand upon

Billy's forehead. She spoke his name and, miracle of miracles, the childish eyes opened and a smile flickered over the pain-twisted little face.

The doctor brought a chair and placed it beside the bed for Nina, while he regarded her admiringly.

Martha drew away from beside the Reverend. There was a world of unspoken resignation in the movement. She moved towards Nina, near enough to grasp the girl's brown hand with fervor.

Young Reverend Duncan remained where he was, a little apart from the waiting group about the bed, though from his position, Nina's profile shone in clear perspective and her tilted nose made such an alluring study that he forgot his straying propensity to delight in Martha's charms.

Isn't there some old adage about "*all's well that ends well*"? Mother Upton decided there was as she serenely set herself to bake another of her huge, mellow, yellow meated cakes for the coming Sunday night's supper.

Half-Century Magazine 7 (Aug. 1919): 4.

The Nettleby's New Years

"BY THE WAY, PHOEBE, what have we on for New Year's?" Phoebe unwound a length of thread from a spool before answering. "We'll have a dinner party; the Sanderson's and Mayme and Gordon are coming. Have you anyone else in mind, Peter, you've asked that question three times."

Peter's face was hidden behind the evening paper, so Phoebe could not see that his expression belied his words.

"Oh, I'm just eager for a pre-war New Year's spread, that's all." Phoebe hummed softly to herself as she busily stitched up a rent in a large gay-colored ball. Peter Junior sprawled on a rug at her feet.

Peter lowered his paper and gazed pridefully upon the pair, a moment, then his face clouded again and with an air almost comical in its assumed carelessness, flung out, "Why-er, have you seen Aunt Pinkie lately?"

Phoebe, intent upon her task, murmured, "Who?"

Encouraged by her lack of interest, Peter repeated more stoutly, "Have you seen Aunt Pinkie lately?"

"No; and when I think of their uncouthness and those two unruly children, I have no wish to see them."

Peter somewhat hurriedly resumed his reading, while Phoebe happily unaware of his discomfiture, hummed merrily and stitched away on her baby's ball. Finally, the ball finished, Phoebe tossed it to Peter Junior who received it with a joyful crow; the signal for Peter and Phoebe to join in a romp, chasing the gay toy, to return it to the fat little sovereign, sitting in all his dignity upon the rug, cheering them on with squeals of delight. But in spite of the fun, Peter's conscience pricked him. He did want other guests at what was to be Phoebe's grandest dinner party. He wanted the Abbotts.

Silas and Aunt Pinkie and their two children, Ruby Pearl and Freddy, made up the Abbott family, but recently removed from the South. They were of that type of lowly souls, so good at heart, so simple in mind, so childlike in credulity and dogged at toil, who are easily preyed upon by the unjust. Consequently they had drunk copiously of all things bitter in life, for they were not merely poor and unread; but they were Negroes. The greatest good that had ever befallen them was their removal from the South—a happening so haphazard and so unplanned that Silas and his little family had arrived in the Northern city nearly penniless. However, a lucky chance threw them in contact with Peter Nettleby.

Peter had stumbled upon Silas, a raw and ignorant hand at the foundry, rattled and mystified and too shy to ask aid of his more self-reliant mates. Peter at once befriended him. He went to the Abbotts' home and the good will, which he in his strength gave poor, weak Silas, was at once extended to his honest, good-natured wife and their youngsters, little roughnecks, who had won his heart. Overlooking their exterior uncouthness after his first glimpse into their kindly hearts, Peter saw that he could help them and thereupon shouldered the responsibility.

Now Peter had never fully explained to Phoebe all the philanthropic notions he entertained toward every down-and-out member of their race. Excepting the one or two amusing happenings about Silas, which Peter had told her, Phoebe knew next to nothing of the Abbott family. So it was altogether surprising, when one Friday Peter telephoned that he was bringing the Abbotts to dinner. It was an ill-chosen time, Friday always being Phoebe's busiest day. And this day, in particular, had been unusually trying. Peter Junior was cross, and Phoebe had planned a very light supper. Now the message, coming as it did, just a short while in advance of Peter and his guests, quite upset Phoebe. Of course Peter should have known all this and certainly if he had considered he would have realized that one extra person to dinner, if unexpected, is at times confusing, and that four extras would most likely bewilder any housekeeper. But this knowledge, if Peter ever possessed it, faded away before his desire to do something nice for the Abbotts.

Old Mrs. Morrison, who often helped Phoebe, consented to come and assist her with the dinner. But even with help, Phoebe was obliged to work swiftly and in her haste the choicest table-linen was brought out, then recklessly she decided to use it, not knowing how reckless her deed was. But all told, Phoebe pulled through splendidly and was quite ready when a smiling Peter—a Peter absolutely sure that his Phoebe would meet him on his own ground, certain that his little house would look its best, and willing to bet that the forthcoming repast would be one to remember—ushered his guests into her presence.

The guests, they were ludicrous indeed. First came Silas, a little, prematurely old man, whose black face glistened with a nervous perspiration, whose teeth flashed intermittently between his heavy lips in a nervous grin, whose hands, toil-worn and gnarled, flew over his body, from collar to wrist band, in a nervous frenzy, his large feet turned pathetically inward as if to avoid taking up too much space, while his eyes—the wistful eyes of a child—pleaded silently for the approbation which would put him at his ease.

There was Pinkie Abbott, short and stout, on the whole quite pleasing to look at, but now standing in her fresh and crisply starched calico dress and immaculate white apron, while on each side of her, at arm's length, she clutched a child by the hand. She walked just in front of where her husband stood and casting defiant, almost sullen glances at her surroundings, she resembled ever so much an angry mother-hen defending her brood.

Dangling from her mother's right hand, Baby Pearl, a chubby little girl, tugged and twisted; tight little braids stood at attention over her head. A bulging forehead shadowed her bright little eyes and impish gleams shot from them—gleams that were as surprising as the sudden flash of a night-light. Grasping his mother's left hand, Freddy, an equally chubby little boy, swung himself forward and back, using his mother's arm as a pendulum. His forehead bulged like his sister's and his eyes, if such could be possible, were brighter and far more impish.

Nothing but the insurmountable instinct of race, which only a traitor can submerge, caused Phoebe to welcome them, for the Abbotts were as unlike the Nettlebys as the moon in her soft radiance is unlike the sun's garish light. That was a never-to-be-forgotten dinner. To dainty Phoebe it was a nightmare; to soft-hearted Peter, it was a painful exhibition of the outcome of years and years of suppression and limited opportunity; and to the Abbotts it was a long drawn-out torture through which they sputtered and gulped. Phoebe's fine table linen with its numerous daubs and stains bore silent testimony to the hard struggle of the Abbotts and their children at that ne'er forgotten feast.

When the Abbotts left, Peter's face was truly woebegone, so Phoebe did not scold about the confusion he had caused her and nothing whatever was said then or afterwards about their guests. Only several days later Phoebe found a crisp banknote pinned beside her place at the table which was lovable Peter's way of telling her to replace her ruined linen.

⊱✦⊰

WINTRY WINDS, despite the fact that it was the holiday season, did not fail to bring their usual supply of colds and croups. An evening or two after Christmas, on which Peter had remained in town with friends, Peter Junior quite suddenly, without previous warning, developed a hoarseness. With alarming swiftness he became worse, until a distraught Phoebe telephoned for Peter to come at once and bring a doctor.

Phoebe was along with her baby and already little Peter was beginning to breathe with the choking indrawn noise of croup. It was terrifying. Despite any arguments advanced, babies need their grandmothers; the first babies especially, are in need of these sweet old ladies who delight in pooh-poohing away the young mother's theories and rejoice in proving that they are still expert at the world-old task of taking care of babies. But poor Phoebe had no such solace and she was frightened out of her wits. It seemed that Peter would never come. Then the door-bell rang with the suddenness of an alarm, accompanied by a halloo, as out of place as a chimney on a tireless cooker, though it served its purpose for it told Phoebe that Pinkie Abbott was at her door.

Relief shone in Phoebe's eyes, for in another minute Pinkie Abbott had entered the room. Some snow still clung to her boots, which she shuffled off onto Phoebe's polished floor. But it went unnoticed, for now the barrier was down and Phoebe entrusted her child to the capability of the older woman.

"I declare, Mrs. Nettleby, that child's sick—croup, too—I declare to goodness seem's if everybody's sneezing and coughing. It sure is lucky I dropped in to see you. It ain't long ago, I 'lowed to Silas, how I was itching to do something to show how we appreciate you-alls kindness to us. Lord, Mrs. Nettleby, me and Silas ain't up in no educated ways, but we sure know when anybody does us a good turn. And you-alls sure been a God-sent blessin' to us. I believes the Lord sent me away out here this evening 'cause I certainly knows a lot about children. I nussed all of Mrs. Hampton's five and every once in so often I've been called here and there to lend a hand. But I declare—" here Pinkie Abbott began to shake in silent merriment, "I declare, what's the use of all that long commendation, when there's my own Ruby Pearl and Freddy to show for themselves what I am at nussing. Silas can say for one thing, that none of his money ever goes to any of your no-count doctors. I treats our ailments myself and it ain't none too often that anything ails us."

While she talked, Pinkie Abbott, with the sureness of the adept, anointed warmed flannels and applied them to Peter Junior. She sniffed at the various things she found in Phoebe's medicine cabinet and asked for mutton-tallow. Then she discussed at great length the efficacy of mutton-tallow and goose-grease. At some time during her chatter, to Phoebe's great relief, Peter Junior's long, indrawn breaths subsided into peaceful breathing. It was Pinkie Abbott, also, who having tucked the baby into his crib, placed her arms akimbo, while her sides shook and her kind eyes twinkled and her pearly teeth gleamed in laughter, said to Phoebe, "Ah, you sure's a 'fraid-cat, honey—but then we all is with our first—I remembers—" and she launched into a wonderful yarn which kept Phoebe amused until Peter came with the doctor.

⊰⧊⊱

PHOEBE, always impulsive, could think of nothing to atone for her somewhat lofty attitude towards the Abbotts than a cordial invitation to her New Year's party.

Pinkie Abbott accepted in what seemed to be a pleased fashion, before going away with the doctor, who promised to take her home in his car. Peter wisely kept his counsel, and stoutly declared that all the Abbotts needed was the right sort of contact, and he had wanted with all his generous heart, to have them at his New Year's feast.

But Phoebe, like all impulsive persons, regretted her act the next morning, nor could you blame her, because the Abbotts would be certain to cut ridiculous figures before the fashionable Sandersons, the up-to-date Mayme, and the fastidious Gordon Moss. Yet having made the plunge, there was no way in which she could back out.

A day or two later, Mrs. Abbott called again on pretense of seeing Peter Junior. But Phoebe knew by her manner that some other reason prompted the visit; yet she was unprepared for the flood of emotion which Mrs. Abbott let loose as soon as she was seated.

"Oh, Mrs. Nettleby," she cried earnestly, "I don't want to come to no more of your high-toned dinner parties, neither me nor Silas nor the children; no ma'am, Mrs. Nettleby, we don't. Now please don't be 'fended at us for it does seem's if my family ain't never goin' to have no happiness like other folks no matter how hard we works and strives. All my life, even when I was a young'un, I used to say, one of these days I was goin' to have a real Christmas with all the blessed fixin' I'd ever seen any body else have on Christmas, a tree with candles on it, and presents, and a dinner, and a real New Year's with a dinner and friends to the house. Lands, Mrs. Nettleby, I was born on New Year's and so was Ruby Pearl, and even in my dreams I've seen that dinner—turkey, cranberries, stuffing, baked ham, sweet potatoes, pone, greens, and a fancy salad, and nuts, fruits, and cakes all iced, and pies—um-um-um—whole stings of 'em—and before the Lord, Mrs. Nettleby, you has to eat some of my coconut pie to know what I mean by pie."

The elder woman paused for breath and though she smiled at Phoebe, her eyes were wistful, but Phoebe was glowing with inspiration.

"Yes ma'am, Mrs. Nettleby," Pinkie Abbott continued, "You ain't got no sort of notion how I've wanted to have a real dinner right in my own home, fixed with my own two hands for my own precious family. Land sakes, no invited-to-dinner New Year's is ever goin' to suit me, until I have the one I want at home—not me, who all my life's been away from home during the holidays, packing and toting for someone else. It ain't that I haven't seen a real one—Lord, Lordy, I've seen 'em a plenty. I've seen trees fixed up so's they dazzle your eyes, but that ain't it. They weren't mine. I didn't get no 'joyment out'n looking at 'em 'cause my own little ones were at home alone, a waiting for their pappy and me, and all Old Santa could ever find to bring them was some old doll made out of my old petticoat or some old 'lassas candy."

Phoebe's glowing eyes were moist as she bent nearer to put her arm about Aunt Pinkie's shoulder. "Aunt Pinkie," she whispered, "You didn't have a real Christmas this year, but suppose we have that real New Year's."

Pinkie Abbott gasped. What could it mean? Astonishment spread over her face, revealing the greatness of her desire, then slowly her eyes shed their unbelief when she saw that Phoebe was in earnest. She became loquacious in explaining her plans and took on that unattached gleam, which comes when hope is gratified.

In less than no time, Phoebe had a description of the doll Ruby Pearl wanted, of the tool chest Freddy had hoped for. She knew the size gloves Silas wore and just how large the turkey had to be.

How the next three days flew by; how they revealed to Phoebe the happiness that comes with service; how they harkened the heavy hearts of Silas and his family and brought the real spirit of the season in all its shining glory to dwell in the Nettleby home. Phoebe spent most of the time with the Abbotts. She had but little money left from her Christmas shopping but she had what is better still—a desire to help and plenty of love. She took the tree she had trimmed for the baby and placed it in the Abbotts' small parlor. Most of the holly wreaths that had gleamed from the Nettlebys' windows glistened instead in the Abbotts'.

New Year's morning little Ruby Pearl hugged a big brown-skinned, curly-haired doll to her bosom and cried in an odd, unchildlike manner from sheer joy. Fat little Freddy manfully strove to hide his delight in a tool chest by viciously driving imaginary nails into the roll of carpet at his feet.

That carpet, green with glaring scrolls of red, had caused Peter to wear his old suit another season, but the appeal in Silas Abbott's eyes had done it when he accosted Peter with, "She's done worked so hard."

Silas himself had gloves—warm ones adorned with fur—and the dinner was all that even Aunt Pinkie had hoped for, but Phoebe, though she didn't mind it at all, had to go without the new hat and set of furs she had planned to buy at the annual January clearance sale.

Half-Century Magazine 8 (Jan. 1920): 5, 14–15.

Jack Arrives

JACK DERBY was a likeable sort, a good mixer, a dandy talker, and a splendid worker. When he married Clarice Winston every one of his friends declared he was bound to be successful, for who with his trade, his disposition and a pretty little wife could not succeed, was an unanswerable question.

Jack married shortly after finishing his course at the Maxwell Mechanical Arts School. In fact as soon as he finished he secured a position with the firm of Sears, Contractors and Builders. It was a fair position for the head of a newly made family of two; but it would not pay if the family increased, and it would go but a short way towards showing off a successful man. But of course, Jack did not intend to be a stationary piece of furniture in his employer's office. His well-wishers kept on saying complimentary things about him while they watched and waited for him to "show 'em."

One, two, three, four years passed over Jack's head as slick as a cowboy's toss of a lasso, and he still drew the same pay-check; also to the casual observer, there was no discernible change in his pleasing demeanor. Though, of course, everyone knew that now, when he went home at night, a small, pert chap, a saucy miniature of himself, climbed onto his knee and called him Daddy. And a close observer could see that a great deal of his sang froid had disappeared and a steady gleam pierced the friendly light in his eyes, which plainly showed how continuously he pondered the problem of living.

In fact, his problems were becoming quite unsolvable with the afore-mentioned check. The way Junior paddled out his little boats, the manner in which his knee protruded through diverse stockings and ye gods! the way he burst out of his little blue jeans, was certainly one vast problem.

Worrying over problems is a joke at all times, and pondering them is debatable, since nothing on earth ponders more on the job than an ass, so when all is said and done, a fellow must get out and hustle if he really wishes to hear success buzz in his ear. Yet it is funny how the really little things, more or less, throw the die in a man's destiny. In Jack's case it was the sugar bowl.

Clarice, Jack's wife, was a sweet little thing, clever as could be, and as cheery as a sunbeam, but she was forgetful. She had a sort of comical forgetfulness too, for instance, she never forgot Jack's favorite dishes but sometimes she would forget to put the salt into one or the sage in another. And this particular morning her forgetfulness had to do with the sugar bowl.

When Jack and Clarice and Junior sat down to breakfast, Jack reached for the sugar bowl but found the bowl empty. Clarice had forgotten to fill it. Seeing this, she sprang up and darted into the kitchen headed for the sugar can on its shelf. She took it down, but alas, it, also, was empty. She had forgotten to order sugar.

Clarice was a winsome little body and never had she appeared more so than now when she skipped back into the dining room, with the empty sugar bowl in her hand. But for once in his life, Jack overlooked her winsomeness as he spied the still empty receptacle for sugar . . . then the storm broke.

Jack wasn't entirely to blame since his nerves were already strained to the breaking point due to the many sugar restrictions he had undergone in recent years. Yet there was no necessity for his raving throughout the meal because he had no sugar. He declared he was growing poorer every day, couldn't afford an ounce or two of sugar—the idea—he would quit his job, leave the town, go elsewhere and find decent employment that would afford him a living wage. Now the more he raved and ramped, the more imbued he became with these propositions which sprang as it were from an empty sugar bowl.

Finally the clock struck the hour for him to go. Then as he hurriedly stooped to kiss Clarice good-bye, the tear drop which trickled alongside her nose fell upon his face and he found that she was crying. And to be sure, woman-like as soon as Clarice knew that he had observed it, her tears started afresh. And Jack could not for worlds, leave his own dear little wifey in tears. Then besides there was Junior, who had hopped down from his place, climbed into his mother's lap and poked his head up, just far enough to become entangled in the embrace Jack was giving Clarice, so here it was, a regular family mixup.

By the time Jack was free to go, the car he should have taken was gone, no jitney in sight, no time could be lost, and the only thing for him to do was to foot it. In short, Jack reached the office a full hour late. Mr. Lashney, the manager, with severity due mostly to surprise, reprimanded Jack sharply, which Jack resented with an equal sharpness. As you probably know, the sequence of such things is either retreat or fire. And Jack skillfully maneuvered the former.

He rushed home with an air of bravado which he certainly did not feel. Then little Clarice assumed that pure, unalloyed bravery that all good women display when their menfolk are in need. And together they reconnoitered their field of attainment, and the inventory of their resources revealed a paltry bank account, a capital stock of good health and a fine reserve fund of good spirits—nothing more.

After this a week was spent in seeing Clarice and Junior comfortably situated and their household goods in storage, and Jack set off in quest of fortune, success, or if you like—simply a job.

The weeks flew into months and the months spun into a year, swiftly as a boy's top spinning upon its peg, yet Jack had not found the position which would put him on his feet. Instead he found that his nut-brown face, his black friendly eyes and his big smiling mouth were more potent than leprosy in chasing away the jobs which might have been his.

Every ounce of his old-time cheeriness vanished as time after time the work for which he was fitted was denied him. Finally, he worked at any and all sorts of odd jobs in one town after another, to get together the monthly allowance to send to Clarice and Junior.

It was a rainy afternoon; Jack had walked all over the town of Ferndale looking for work. Even his reserve fund of good spirits had sprung a leak and began to dribble away, when on passing a newsstand he spied his favorite trades magazine and stopped to purchase a copy of it. He went back to his dingy little room to pore over the periodical and in so doing, forget the many disappointments the year had held for him.

Jack loved his work next best to his wife and baby. Back of the friendly laughter in his eyes slumbered visions of beautiful creations in wood and stone. His strong long fingers never tired of making sketches on paper, and his brain worked indefatigably on foundations and wainscots and windows; "a born architect," was the verdict passed upon him by his old associates in the firm of Sears, Contractors and Builders.

Now his fingers turned the leaves almost caressingly as he read them one after another. Then, what? . . . a whole page devoted to an advertisement of a contest. His perfunctory glancing changed as he read in keen interest and when he had finished, he closed the book and looked out from his window over the house-tops off into space where smoky rain-clouds huddled against the sky like downy chicks and the glow of a dream darkened his eyes.

Jack's ambition led to a far-off pinnacle whereon he would be able to establish himself as an architect—when people would come from far and near to have him plan their homes and cities would bid him come to plan their public buildings—then, ah then, his bread and butter secure, he would build as he chose and in long years to come, others would look upon his work and see not mere bricks and stones, but the beautiful soul of an artist, for in all of his work he would weave one of his lovely dreams. And that which he had read caused his ambition to right about-face and marshal his dreams together. Again he scanned the page:

$10,000.00

TO BE GIVEN FOR SOMETHING DIFFERENT

$10,000.00

To Any One

SUBMITTING PLANS FOR A BUNGALOW

which meets the approval of

MRS. WAGNER-ANHAUSER

CONTEST OPEN TO ALL

Send Sketch and Plans for Bungalow to

HALLOWELL & HALLOWELL

Contest Closes January 1st, 1920

Jack held his breath. Could he dare to hope and even then Hope's dancing fires were in his eyes.

In a further perusal of the magazine, Jack saw a brief write-up of Mrs. Wagner-Anhauser, a lady of vast wealth, a direct descendant of the famous composer and the equally famous brewer, and Jack smiled as he whimsically thought how the artistic and commercial nature of Mrs. Wagner-Anhauser was revealing itself in this blatant method of securing a home. Nevertheless if he could only pluck the substantial, tempting morsel she was holding out—ah if—and again Jack held his breath.

The afternoon drizzle had changed into snow and the ground was covered with a thick slush when Jack set out again. He went to a telegraph office and sent a message:

Clarice, dear, send the blue-print of dream house at once. JACK.

Even before Jack and Clarice married they had amused themselves planning the kind of bungalow they would build when "dreams came true." After they were married and had found out numerous little kinks in housekeeping, Jack had playfully added corners and cupboards and cabinets and rooms and always with his instinct for beauty uppermost, until now their "dream house," as they called it, was a little marvel of beauty and convenience. And this, Jack decided to send to Hallowell & Hallowell.

He had only a short time to wait for the outcome of the contest and while he waited he remained in his little dingy room and to make ends meet he went to work with a bullying contractor, the clod hopper kind, who contracts to erect a building and afterwards portions this work out to any and as many jack-legged carpenters and bricklayers as he can obtain cheaply. To be sure, an ordeal for Jack, but most of his work was in the open. It was in that delightful season of the year when a golden haze suspends itself like a veil from earth to sky; when the evening's layer of snow or the night's hoar frost is vanished by a warm noon-day sun. A time to dream and hope.

It was the end of a dreamy day in March and Jack was somewhat uneasy about Clarice and Junior. When he received his last letter from them, Junior was ill and several days had passed without any other further word. He was horribly tired. The workmen had loitered more than usual and their boss had given full vent to his angry bellowing. He entered his little room wearily and switched on a light. Then his eyes fell upon two letters lying together on a table. His kindhearted landlady had placed them there. One was from Clarice and the other bore the firm address of Hallowell & Hallowell in the upper right-hand corner. This he tore open with feverish hands and read the words which leapt and danced as the paper trembled in his nervous hands. The air in the dingy little room seemed to throb as his emotion vibrated through it.

He stood there silent, staring. Then he spoke aloud, "At last, at last!" With that he shook himself and straightened. Then he wheeled about the room in an ecstasy of happiness. Finally, he stopped before his little sheet iron heater—which was quite cheerily aglow—and spoke.

"Well, well, old boy, this is one on 'em. Why you old black cuss, you've put one over fair and square. Yes siree, and I'll be darned, just the same as if your dad-burned hide was white." Then in comical surprise at his own stupidity his voice changed to say, "Drat it, you simp, why don't you get ready for home?" With these words he began to toss his things together preparing for that event. As he worked his mind sang busily with plans for the future and strangely too, not a single plan had to do with wonderful architectural feats, not one, but all were of a trusting, winsome woman and a bonny little boy and a cheery fire on a cozy hearth.

Now and then he laughed—not the hearty, exultant laughter of him who wins, but the softened throaty laugh of one who loves and yearns, for memories both sweet and fragrant surged through him as his thought flashed back and away to where Clarice and Junior beckoned and called him.

Half-Century Magazine 8 (Feb. 1920): 5, 14.

El Tisico

"WHAT IS PATRIOTISM?" shouted O'Brady, the Irish engineer, as peppery as he was good-natured. He was showing signs of his rising choler faster and faster as the heated argument grew in intensity.

He argued that it was a thing men put before their wives, and Tim held that it couldn't be compared with love-making and women.

"Cut it, boys, and listen to this," broke in Sam Dicks, a grizzled old train-man, who had more yarns in his cranium than a yellow cur has fleas on a zig-zag trail between his left ear and his hind right leg.

"Fire up," roared the crowd of us.

The debate on patriotism had started between O'Brady and Tim Brixtner in the Santa Fé restroom. It was a typical scene—the long paper-strewn table occupying the center space, and sturdy sons of America—hard-muscled, blue chinned, steady-nerved, rail-road men—lounging around it. Over in the alcove, upon a raised platform, three colored men, who styled themselves "The Black Trio," were resting after their creditable performance. They had given us some of the best string music from banjo, mandolin, and guitar I have ever heard.

One of them, a big, strapping, ebony fellow, minus an arm, had a baritone voice worth a million, headed under different color. He sang "Casey Jones"—not a classic—but take it from me, a great one among our kind. He sure sang it. . . .

A colored youngster, whom they carried about with them, had just finished passing the hat. It had been all both hands could do to carry it back to "The Black Trio." I, myself, had flung in five bucks, the price I'd pay, maybe, to go to a swell opera.

The guy who played the banjo was a glowing-eyed, flat-chested fellow with a cough, which he used some frequent.

I lit my pipe, and O'Brady and Brixtner and the rest lit theirs. Sam Dicks was about to begin when the "Trio" showed signs of departing. He left us with, "Wait a bit, boys," and went to them. He gave the glad hand to the glowing-eyed, coughing one, with a genuine friendship grip. He came back ready for us.

"In the early nineties I was working with Billy Bartell, the greatest dare-devil and the squarest that ever guided a throttle. We made our runs through that portion of the country which is sure God's handiwork, if anything is. It always strikes me as being miraculous to see the tropic weather of old Mex and the temperate weather of our U.S., trying to mix as it does along the border. It gives us a climate you can't beat—but the landscape, sun-baked sand, prairie-dog holes, and cactus with mountains dumped indiscriminately everywhere, all covered by a sky that's a dazzle of blue beauty, is what I call God's handiwork, because it can't be called anything else.

"At one of our stops in one of Mexico's little mud cities, a colored family—father, mother, and baby—boarded the train. The woman was like one of those little, pearly-grey doves we shoot in New Mexico, from August to November—a little, fluttery thing, all heart and eyes.

"When they got on, their baby was a mere bundle, so no one noticed its illness. But it was soon all aboard that a sick kid was on. He *was* a sick kid, too: so sick that every mother's son on that train felt sorry and wanted to do something.

"The mother's eyes grew brighter and brighter, and the father kept watching his kid and pulling out his big, gold watch. The baby grew worse.

"In some way, as the intimate secrets of our heart sometimes do, it crept out that the family was trying to get over to the U.S. side before the baby died. We still had an eight-hour run, and the baby was growing worse, faster than an engine eats up coal.

"The mother's eyes scanned the country for familiar signs. Every time I passed through that coach and saw her, I was minded of the way wounded birds beat their wings on the hard earth in an effort to fly. To all our attempted condolence, she replied with the same words:

"'If he lives until we get home—if he lives till we get home.'

"Billy Bartell always knew who his passengers were. He used to say he didn't believe in hauling whole lots of unknown baggage. So he knew that we carried the sick kid. We passed word to him that the kid was worse, and what his parents were aiming for.

"Well, boys, after that, our train went faster than a whirligig in a Texas cyclone. The landscape—cactus, prairie-dog holes, and mountains—rolled into something compact and smooth as a khaki-colored canvas, and flashed past us like sheets of lightning. We steamed into Nogales. The depot was on the Mexican side, but the coach with the sick kid landed fair and square upon American sod.

"The little colored woman with her baby in her arms, alighted on good old American turf. She turned in acknowledgment to the kindness she had received, to wave her hand at the engine and its engineer, at the coaches and all the passengers, at everything, because she was so glad.

"If the kid died, it would be in America—at home."

Old Dicks paused a moment before querying, "Boys, did you get it?"

"You bet," spoke up Brixtner. "That's patriotism. Now, Pat O'Brady! 'Twasn't no man and woman affair either," he cried, eager to resume their interrupted debate.

"Wait a minute, fellows," pleaded Dicks, "wait."

"I want to know, did the kid live?" somebody asked.

"That's what I want to tell," said Dicks.

"Eh, you, Tim! Cut it, cut it. . . ."

"That little banjo picker was the kid whose parents did not want him to die out of sight of the Stars and Stripes."

A long-drawn "phew" fairly split the air—we were so surprised.

"Yes," said he, "and he has never been well, always sick. He's what the Mexicans call, 'el Tisico.'"

"Scat. . . . He isn't much of a prize!"

"What's he done to back up his parents' sentiments?"

"He sure can't fight." These were the words exploded from one to the other.

"Do you know what 'The Black Trio' do with their money?" asked Dicks, pride modulating his voice.

"Well—I—guess—not," drawled someone from among the bunch.

"Every red cent of it is turned in to the American Red Cross—do you get me?" And old Dicks unfolded the evening paper and began to read.

"Be Gad, that's patriotism, too," shouted O'Brady. "Can any son-of-a-gun define it?"

Crisis 19 (March 1920): 252–253.

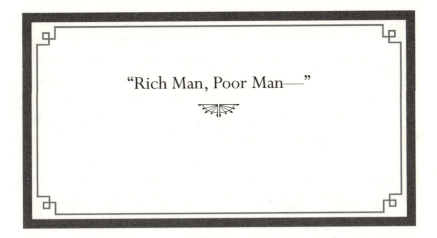

"Rich Man, Poor Man—"

DRUSILLA EVANS was a rich man's daughter. Old big black double-jointed Daniel Evans was her father. So big was he, that he towered above every other man in the community; so black, that his genial wrinkled old countenance shone strikingly wherever he went; and so shrewd and industrious was he that the Evans ranch and the Bar-Crescent-E brand was as widely known as other longer standing ones like the Diamond D and the X—Z outfits.

Drusilla's mother was just such a woman as most sure-footed men choose for a partner. A tall, slender woman was she, with a delicate, fragile air—a woman with soft warm eyes and a gentle voice and a smiling mouth above the roundest, stubbornest chin.

Drusilla herself was just such a daughter as one would expect to spring from such a well-matched team as old Daniel and his wife. She was sparklingly pretty, a jolly twinkling star of a girl. And because she was so pretty and perhaps because she was so rich, the suitors she had in tow were not to be numbered. However, gossip said it would be a long time ere Drusilla married, for who, pray, would be able to match old Daniel's dollars, and wouldn't Drusilla be a fool to marry a poor man?

One of the main impressions of Drusilla's childhood coincided with this line of gossip. Day in and day out, her father's friends had gathered in her home of evenings to partake of old Daniel's hospitality. They played cards at times, but the main business of these little gatherings had been to talk—and how they talked. Sometimes politics, sometimes religion; at times a long drawn-out tale of Indian War days, but the one sincere, palpably sincere argument was the Race Question discussed again and again and over and over.

In red headlines some paper would herald some atrocity done a Negro—always some unknown, far-off Negro; but the little band of black men gathered in the Evans parlor were wont to discuss it pro and con in subdued and sorrowful voices.

From listening to these talks, Drusilla had learned to know and honor Douglass, Washington, Cuney and Langston. She knew and admired the race benefactors and having heard the race haters like Vardaman, Tillman and Dixon, Jr., ridiculed with true American humor, she was able to laugh her jolly, twinkling laughter at their piteously self-belittling antics.

Often the men would bring their wives and then the women joined with the men in a friendly combat with words. Race men, versus race women, was the topic of the day whenever this occurred, and one of these arguments had stuck and sprouted like a seed in fertile soil in Drusilla's mind.

"Now men, you know," one of the women would declare, "our menfolk are slack about letting their wives work—" That would start the bout.

"Work—Work," little peppery Mr. Stinson would shout. "What can we do—how's a man to support a wife and children on the mere pittance he gets a day?"

"Get a job that pays more than a pittance," some crisp tongued woman would return.

"Indeed, indeed, wouldn't we, if we could. A black woman can always get a good (?) job in somebody's kitchen, but a black man can't get a good (?) job cleaning the streets; if some white man happens to want it."

Now Drusilla as a very little, twinkly star of a girl decided that no matter what came or went—she would not work for any man alive.

"When I marry," she would say, "my man is going to take care of me." Then she would quote a remembered fragment from some of the old arguments. "It's a sorry man who can't take care of his own family."

Then came a day when Drusilla's sparkling prettiness forgot to twinkle and glowed and shone instead. Drusilla's mother discovered it first. It had been she who first likened Drusilla to a twinkling star. Long ago, when Drusilla was a wee mite, Mrs. Evans had held her close in her arms while looking into her sparkling eyes and chanted the old nursery rhyme:

"Twinkle, twinkle, little star, how I wonder what you are?" And the little Drusilla had answered: "Why muvver, I'm your little daughter." So now that she no longer twinkled, Mrs. Evans was the first to notice.

Drusilla came in one evening after she and a party of young folk had been on a hike to the mountains. John Condon had been with them—John Condon, young and as poor as a church mouse, possessing a lovableness utterly compelling, working at the menial task of chauffeuring, and newly arrived from the East in the train of his wealthy Eastern employers.

"Oh Daughter," Mrs. Evans had exclaimed, "my little girl."

Then Drusilla had walked straight into her mother's arms and hidden her starry glowing face on her mother's bosom, and both had cried a little and gazed into each other's face, wet-eyed and trustingly.

Said Mrs. Evans, "Daughter, John is a poor man, a poor black man, daughter; have you thought of that."

"Yes, yes," cried Drusilla, "but John can make his way."

"So he can, Daughter, if you are willing to help." But little Drusilla, shocked through and through, sprang up at this, crying: "Why mother, I wouldn't work for any man alive. John shall make his way alone."

"Daughter," returned Mrs. Evans, "you do not know how your father got the money to buy our first cow. I'll tell you. I, your mother, did day work, washed and scoured from house to house. That cow, a heifer, cost us thirty-five dollars, and it took me two solid months to earn enough to get her."

"Oh Mother," exclaimed Drusilla, pityingly. Then brightly, "But times have changed. So I'm not going to wash and scour for John Condon, cows or no cows."

Mrs. Evans smiled understandly, and little Drusilla snuggled down beside her, and they sat down together with their arms entwined, silently, knowing they had reached the bitter-sweet moment that comes to every mother and every daughter who reaches the parting of their ways.

Said old Daniel Evans to young John Condon a day or two later:

"I want you to know, son, that I've liked you from the first moment I set eyes on you. Though I hadn't figured on you taking my little girl away from me, but—" old Daniel crinkled his black genial face into a whimsical smile and continued: "You know that everything I possess goes to my little girl, too, don't you?" Old Daniel asked the blunt question unexpectedly, and young John fidgeted under the surprise of it; but his eyes so boyish and straightforward, met the older man's unflinchingly, and he answered, "Yes Sir."

"All right, then," resumed old Daniel. "I'm going to tell you something most people do not know. I don't intend to choke the manhood out of any man with my money." He paused, and a full moment elapsed before he spoke again. "I love my little girl, son—so well that you can rest assured that if you never make good, she and her little ones, if there be any, aren't ever going to suffer—no, never, so long as old Dan Evans is in full possession of his strength and mind. But I'd die mighty happy, son, if I had some way of knowing that the man she'd tied to was a man—that the family she was a-building was being built on rock foundation. When I'm gone every cent goes to my children; but figuring on their chances compared to what I had, my children ought to leave their children a fortune treble the value of mine. Sounds like a Chinese puzzle, boy; but what have you to say?"

Old Dan laughed heartily, and grasped the youth's shoulder, swung him about easily and looked into his face. "Is it a go, my girl, but not a red cent goes with her, not one red cent until you have proved your metal. I'll fit up a little house right nigh my own—"

"Oh, no you don't," interrupted John. "I'm in love with your daughter, but not with your West. When we are married, back East for us."

"What? Well, it's all right, son, but it pricks my hope bubble. I'd set my heart on keeping my little girl close."

Of course Drusilla's friends were aghast when they heard of her engagement. Their own dear little Drucy going to marry a poor nobody. The idea. The overly-wise young fellows about town on hearing it winked their eyes, cocked their heads to one side, exhaled pungent cigarette smoke through their burnt-out nostrils, and gave vent to much conjecture; namely, "How the deuce had that Eastern fish managed to hook in all that money?"

Nevertheless, John and Drusilla were married and went away to make a home of their own. John with very high hopes, indeed, for was not he taking with him as a bride, the prettiest, sweetest girl on earth? world? In little cozy moments when they were alone, Drusilla would say, "John, dear, I'd die for you." And John would say gaily, joyously, "Right, o'right girl, but just keep on living, won't you?"

All this was very well and good, and yet better, John found a cute little nest of a house and eventually another job as chauffeur in a private family. They were very happy. Drusilla cooked spicy, tasty little dishes, and kept them piping hot for supper, which was a variable affair owing to John's employment. She kept their tiny rooms shining like mirrors and her own pretty self as trim and neat as a rose-bud.

But the butcher, the grocer, the rent, the fuel—the bills climbed up amazingly, and at the end of a month when they were all paid, what was left of John's wages looked like a small boy's Christmas gift from a maiden aunt.

John worked like a galley-slave. He added the care of several offices to his other tasks. He grew lean as a foxhound. In his spare moments he was far too tired to play around with Drusilla. He would even forget to tell her how pretty she looked, or how good the supper tasted. This of course aroused a vague uneasiness within Drusilla. Yet, needless to say, the remarks that she had heard on every side concerning John's poverty, and the solicitude which well-meaning friends bestowed upon her before her marriage all had their effect. Indeed, she considered John's effort to make ends meet, an acknowledgment of the sacrifice she had made to become his wife.

Then something happened. One day, as John, about to take a dangerous curve with his usual careful precision, another chauffeur who knew next to nothing about carefulness, and had no preciseness whatever, took it from the opposite direction with a devil-may-care recklessness. There was a smash-up. Every one of the occupants of John's car were more or less shaken and John was painfully cut by flying glass from his broken wind-shield. They sent for Drusilla from the hospital where John had been carried.

It was a very frightened and contrite Drusilla who was ushered into her husband's presence. Her first impulse had been to send an S.O.S. call to her doting parents; but the first glimpse of dear old John's bandaged face which revealed better than anything else could have done, the square line of his determined chin, with its distracting cleft peeping out beneath the folds of gauze, dispelled that notion easily.

Perhaps this accident would not have changed things materially, for in a few days John came home from the hospital, still swathed in bandages and rather sore; but fully decided to go to work within the next forty-eight hours had not Influenza quite accommodatingly lent itself to the situation. Ignoring the time-honored rule of the game—

not to strike when a man's down—it took a tenacious hold upon John all bandaged and sore as he was, and gave him a race for his life. During the first few days of his illness, John, who couldn't stand pain any better than a day-old kitten, had to endure so much that his mind rambled and he muttered all sorts of queer odds and ends and bits of nonsense—such as a delirious person can.

Drusilla's eyes would mist with tears as she listened; yet her twinkling laughter would ripple out huskily, then she would flash a look at the clock and glance at the medicine schedule beside her. Lord, she would rather cut off her right arm than to miss that medicine right on the dot. One of the things she kept thinking about was the way John muttered about bread. It puzzled her. "Bread, bread, bread," he would say, then he would begin to count, seemingly endless loaves of bread, bread, bread.

When John's fever spent itself, he began to mend rapidly, and the remainder of the time he passed in bed was like a holiday. It was luxurious, to be sure, to rest among real pillows and fall asleep, to awake with nothing on hand to do, other than locating Drusilla, who, knowing how to amuse a fellow, kept her sparkling self just within range of his waking vision. When he was himself again, Drusilla asked why he had raved so about bread. John smiled at that, and reached for his wife's hand, then he answered:

"Girl dear, I'm not a chauffeur. I've as much love for driving a car as you have for running a washing machine. I'm a baker; got the first taste of it working around a French bakery, when I was a kid, then somehow my folks scraped up enough to send me to a school and I specialized in baking. The one thing I've wanted is to own a bakery shop. I bummed around a great deal after I left school, trying to find an opening; but my trade seemed to be the garden of roses for Germans and Bohemians and nobody's even give me a chance to keep the ovens hot. To come down to brass tacks, I had to live so I capitalized on buzz-cars, and oh, girl, you know I'm the nifty kid at the steering-wheel."

Drusilla often ran out to purchase a loaf of bread, or a pie from the little bakery around the corner, owned by a florid-faced German and his round-tub of a wife. The round-tub of a wife was a friendly soul, and always chattered with Drusilla; yet John's good angel must have prompted her to speak thus, a day or two later:

"Mein Gott, the trade's fallen off dreadfully. Mein Gott to think we are Americans, but our looks are the German, so no one comes to buy."

Said Drusilla, quick as a flash, "Turn over your business to me." The smooth brown braids of the German woman and Drusilla's curly tresses mingled as their heads bowed to make speedy calculations over the counter.

"Two hundred and fifty dollars, my dear," exclaimed the proprietress; "two hundred and fifty dollars down and one hundred every six months and the shop, also the little delivery cart, is yours with the blessing of Mein Gott."

Drusilla forgot her parcel, left it lying upon the counter and ran into her own spick and span little house. She went straight into her room, never stopping until she ransacked her belongings, disclosing a veritable garden of gay little dresses; some of these she sorted out and made into a neat pile, saying, "Lovely dresses, you are quite the thing for a rich man's daughter, but you are outlandish for a poor man's wife, so I'm going to sell you to the second-hand man, and tonight I'm going to have $250." Then she laughed gaily, thinking how lucky she was to be in an Eastern city wherein a second-hand clothing shop could be found. She was exceedingly busy all the afternoon, and John having yet to remain indoors, wondered why she did not come to entertain him as she had been doing.

Late that evening Drusilla burst into his presence. Excitement made her sparkling prettiness a dazzling thing to see. She brushed aside John's compliments and rushed on to what she had to say.

"John, dear, haven't I always told you, I'd die for you?"

"You bet," responded he. Drusilla laughed her twinkling laugh, and said, "Well, I've changed my mind. Instead, I'm going to work for you."

John sat up at that, and said harshly, "Yes, I guess not. No woman will ever remember working for me. I'm a man who wants only a man's chance—a man's chance, do you hear, and I'll do the man's part, I'll—"

"John, John," laughed Drusilla, "Will you listen to me?"

Then, as John leaned back among the pillows, Drusilla told him all about her business venture. He could only gasp and stare.

Said she, "It's you and I for the night work, until we get on our feet. Of days, you can peddle our wares in that little antediluvian Ford and I'll sell them over the counter."

"Oh girl," said John, "that means you will have to work. . . ."

"Yes, boy, I've always said I wouldn't work for any man alive, but I've found the one I'm willing to work with."

Then altogether irrelevant to the business in hand, John repeated ever so softly: "Twinkle, twinkle little star . . ." as he put his arms around Drusilla and drew her close.

Half-Century Magazine 8 (May 1920): 6, 14.

Pot Luck

A Story True to Life

LIFE IS A CAPRICIOUS WOMAN who delights to twist awry the threads with which man weaves the tapestry of his existence. She dresses love like a merry little elf and sends him to meet a dusky nurse-maid in a tower garden or she rolls love in the mud and sends him a sordid little imp to intrigue a queen in her court. She flavors her broth with wondrous herbs and condiments and skims off the top, which is tasteless, giving it to those who receive first serving, while those who chance on pot-luck are given the strength of her porridge. She juggles men together, mixes them, shuffles them as a dealer his cards and no one wonders who plays her game if the loser draws a full house and the winner holds a rotten, rotten hand.

Life was capricious to say the least when she tangled the thread in the fabric of Mrs. John Borden's career by snapping the cords which kept Mr. Borden suspended on this earth and tumbling him into eternity, thereby forcing his widow, a hitherto comfortably cared for wife, to take in washing to eke out a scanty livelihood for herself and three-year-old daughter.

Mrs. John Borden with a resignation quite unbelievable in one so fed-up on a diet of petted and cared-for wifedom submitted to life's whims and became a sweating and grim-faced washwoman.

Life smiled complacently as she viewed Mrs. Borden sweating over her tubs, decided nonchalantly to keep her there, and passed on.

Widow Borden, the supposedly meek, spat at her passing and determined that Life, Life the capricious lady, herself, should be made to push the finest of plush upholstered perambulator in which Anne, Mrs. Borden's own daughter, should ride.

An unwise determination to be sure—a veritable flying into the face of destiny—a silly jumping from hot skillet into fire, but nevertheless, a determination that calls for the fortitude of a God and the patience of a saint. Just think of it, resolving to make Life, the capricious woman, push someone in a perambulator. As yet no man has ever conceived such a thing and no woman save only she, whose womanhood is set with the priceless gem of maternity.

This determination, deeply rooted in her motherly bosom, squared Mrs. Borden's shoulders and furnished stamina for her ceaseless toil. At night when her back twinged with pain and her arms swung like dead weights from their sockets the flaming glory of it, like the colors from a golden sunset, flared before her tired eyes causing her to forget the numbing weariness of her aching body and lulling her to sleep. Then of days as she would glance over her steaming tubs and behold little Anne at play at a distance just far enough to be undefiled by soapy suds and dirty linens, the glory of her determination would scintillate and shine like many diamonds and the sound of soiled clothing being rubbed against the rough washboard was as a mighty paean sung in its honor.

Life smiled derisively as she passed.

Little Anne thrived and grew. Grew fast like a fast-growing flower. School demanded her presence, and Widow Borden deprived of her constant pleasure—which was to pause unnumbered times with her arms half hidden in soapy suds supporting the weight of her bending body, while she gazed adoringly upon a dusky child at play—

fell to planning small surprises against Anne's homecoming—the dough for sugar cookies was made overnight while Anne slept, cut out and baked in the intervals when clothes steamed or irons heated, or a gay hair-bow was surreptitiously purchased to be pinned beside a pillow or hidden beneath a plate.

Following swiftly the time arrived, when Anne was no longer short-skirted and easily pleased with a sugar cake fashioned like the badly done caricature of a man. She was grown tall and slim and her skirts swished against her slender ankles. Forthwith Widow Borden advertised for more "Fine Linens" to be "Hygienically Done by Hand." And sent the young Miss off to an expensive, exclusive, gen-teel, finishing school for young ladies.

There, Anne continued her piano lessons. To be sure she had taken music years and years before she could sit and touch the pedals with her toes. Yet even the best of expert teachers failed to teach her any sort of technique. Her greatest endeavors drew from the ivory keys a simple melody, rendered always in too slow a beat.

She studied languages, too, but her French was a woeful pot pourri of unrelated terms, her Spanish was a lob lolly as hard to get away with as a dish of that people's chilli con carne; her Latin, no food combination, Italy's spaghetti or an Irish stew could equal it for a mixture of wasted effort, time, and money. She took up sewing, but they who taught her that domestic art surveyed her crooked hems and puckered tucks with eyes registering horror. For some unknown reason higher mathematics are always taught even in a finishing school for young ladies. Anne's was no exception, but her teachers soon came to know that the well-known and easily done symbol for naught was devised to be used in connection with Anne Borden's work. She had no taste for literature. All the old estimable poems from the time-honored poets, which are usually thrown into the cur-riculum in young ladies' finishing schools, went a-begging with Anne.

Mind you, don't start in blaming Anne. For really she was a peach of a girl, appealing and charming as it is good for a girl to be. She dressed very very fetchingly. Widow Borden with the help of her tubs and washboard saw to that. Her manners were the pink of perfection, and she was entirely kind and lovable.

What more could you ask? In the face of the fact that her father was just a plodding, good-natured colored man, lacking enough forethought to provide for the future welfare of his family, who knew nothing whatever about Longfellow and no less than that about Plato and cared never a fig about either. Her mother, poor soul, used to enjoy listening to Anne strumming, which is to say, she did not know music: and barring her great capacity for unstinted devotion, she was disqualified for everything else in the world, save washing and ironing.

So if any of you expect Life, Life the capricious woman, to pitch her decorum to the winds and do a handspring for the sake of converting the child of a clod-hopping hodcarrier whose mate is a washwoman, into a finished musician or a distinguished linguist, you simply don't know Life. It's far more befitting her caprice to make the sons and daughters of musicians and poets the rag-pickers and scullery maids of tomorrow. If you notice, she takes generations in which to produce and only moments in which to destroy.

But withal, Anne was a real little lady. Didn't some-body say, "that artists and linguists—and cooks—wasn't included—are born?" Leastways, it's a fact. But a lady—bah, a lady—any female who chooses can be that. Take for instance, a little bit of natural inclination, a fair amount of right association, a smattering of education, and a knack at imitation, and you have it.

Life complacently passed on. However outdoing her own capriciousness and quite as Widow Borden willed, condescended to lightly clasp the handle of a fine upholstered perambulator, in which a dusky little lady luxuriously reclined, and shove it along. Eighteen years—Life did just that. Who can say what Life, the capricious woman, will do.

Anne Borden at eighteen was a lovely thing to behold as round and as plump and as merry and carefree as youth when it is cherished and nourished can possibly be. Also, Anne had a gift, you might say half a gift, the gift of song. She could sing liltingly like a bird, warbling as he sits on a dew-drenched vine to watch the sun rise like a golden ball tossed high into the blue bowl of heaven—and as blithely as a boy whistling as he starts off on a coveted half-holiday, headed for his favorite swimming hole. Only, this voice of hers lilting and blithe though it was had not one bit of range, and honest, given a voice like hers and possessing range the Pattises white or black would turn over in their graves.

And again, as a real insight into just the sort of girl Anne was; her class staged the well-known playlet: "Mothers and Babes." In the last act in the role of a young mother bending over a crib, crooning a lullaby, she brought down the house. For her voice had just the right quality of sweetness and the exact quantity of softness to hush babies to sleep and make hardened adults remember their own mother's arms and recall the stilled lullabys of long ago. She brought down the house, I tell you, and the stage floor was literally covered with sweet-young-girl-graduate-bouquets when her act was finished. Mrs. John Borden sitting back out of the way and somewhat hidden by row on row of more pompous and prosperous parents allowed tears—of joy—to flow unheeded down her checks and fall heedlessly upon the real lace jabot dear little Anne had hastily and lovingly pinned about her scrawny neck just before the performance.

THE POST-HASTE METHODS with which joy turns into sorrow and laughter merges into tears would be strange and ridiculous besides being sad; if one did not know that Life is a capricious woman. Hence it was only in keeping with Life's whims that poor self-sacrificing Widow Borden died one short week after accompanying little Anne home from boarding school. All of the meager sum over and above board which had been culled during all the years of hard work was squandered to enable Mrs. Borden's presence upon the memorable occasion; when Anne brought down the house.

It could not have been spent better. It gave Widow Borden the joy of a life-time—it illumined with a dazzling glory the dimming flames of her ambition. It caused the years on years of toil and sacrifice to roll from her tired shoulders like the great waves out at sea. In short she tasted of the sweet honey-dew melon of fulfillment and Life, the capricious woman, who flaunted so many tantalizing gifts, has none to offer more entrancing than that.

Life passed on quite unmindful of the fact that she had unclasped her hands and let go a fine upholstered perambulator that immediately overturned a dusky fairy-like creature in the open highway.

Poor Anne Borden. The question, "What can you do?" was flung at her so often until she smarted with the pain of it as if each word was a cat-o-nine-tails lashed about her body. She was completely befuddled and oh, so helpless.

Then a good old family doctor, a kindly intentioned man; who often intended far kinder things than he ever performed; took her in charge. His intentions toward Anne was kindness itself, but even as he carried her home, he was considering the expense she would be to him. And he was such a poor man; as all doctors know that a sick man grown well makes a hard paymaster. Money was a thing to be thought of, besides his widowed daughter and four lusty grandchildren were dependent upon him. How was he to carry another burden. Quite plainly the thing to do was to get Anne settled as speedily as possible—off his hands anyhow, any way. And at that wouldn't he do a Christian act?

Moodily, he tabulated in his mind different possibilities to get Anne Borden speedily off his hands. The shops near by were closed to her because of color. Theater-goers would scoff at buying tickets from such a dusky maiden. Central, the mecca for girls with pleasing voice and goodly patience, would ring with alarm should so dark an operator strap the gear about her head, put forth her hand to a plug, and call sweetly, "number." He enumerated all the diverse things set aside for the dainty maidens whom Life has teetered downwards and decided they were taboo to Anne Borden on account of a too-brown complexion. And on the other hand all the things accommodatingly tossed to one side for the benefit of dusky maidens down on their luck were likewise out of the question. To wit, no one would be willing to pay Anne Borden to concoct chafing dish delicacies and delectable fudges, not this day and time, when sugar is twenty-eight cents the pound and the very best of us are using oleo-margarine and camouflaging it for butter, no indeed, it requires an old head at the business to stir the pots these days. Laundry work, well I say, the idea. She was not fitted to teach and she could not sew.

Yet there still remains many many things for an untrained person to do. You are right. But remember, Ann Borden was not untrained. She had been actually trained throughout eighteen years to ride in a fine upholstered perambulator. Life had capriciously pushed it. Even Life can carry a joke too far.

A week or two passed in which the good old doctor worked as hard as a sleuth on a mystery case, and finally with the unconscious aid of his grandchildren he was able to place Anne alongside the very pattern Life probably cut out for her use.

The grandchildren had taken to Anne at once. Since her advent among them, they had babbled of no one else. And Anne, poor bereaved creature, secured what solace she was able to get hold of, by occupying the somewhat stormy position of being the center of their attraction.

One day as the old doctor perplexedly stroked his beard and watched Anne with the children all clustered about her, he had an inspiration which revealed itself a couple of days later; when he came in and said to Anne in a manner he considered benign:—

"Get ready, my dear, I've found you a place."

Then with Anne's eyes grown suddenly wide and startled full upon him he was unable to go on in his benign fashion, so he dropped his benignity like peas burst from their shell, and flared out meaningly.

"Come, come, I've found you a place—er—er—a job, you know. Nursing, private family, one child, good pay, good room, a real home you might say, start in at once. Get ready, quickly as you can. We've a long ways to go, across town, 1212 Sonnet's Drive, that's the address. Come, come—"

Anne set to, quickly as she was bidden. And the trunks and bags and boxes, which had so shortly arrived with her from an exclusive and genteel finishing school for young ladies, were piled unto the doctor's rattley old car along with herself and carried across town to 1212 Sonnet's Drive. And so it was that pretty little dusky Anne Borden entered upon the arduous duties of nurse-maid in the home of the Lewis-Osbornes.

Fie fie, a nurse-maid. Widow Borden's dusky little lady. The very Anne, whom Life had allowed to ride in a fine upholstered perambulator, now forced to push a rather sumptuous perambulator herself, containing a husky kicking, red-faced, too-fat, bawling youngster.

Life, Life, you are derisive just as much as you are capricious.

For a long time, Anne suffered sheer martyrdom. Truly was she an alien in a foreign land. She, who in all her days, saving for the fleeting moments on streets and in shops, whence she had glimpsed the haughty visages of another race; had beheld none but the pleasing countenances of her own people. It was worse than bondage, for bondage teaches first of all, to expect any and all indignities; but how was a girl like Anne to know, that because she toiled as nurse-maid she had not even the caste of a bondsman nor the consideration that is given to the family's dog. It had to be learned and her lessons were hard.

Her grief for her mother instead of abating grew more acute with the days and she yearned piteously for the sound of the silent voice and a pressure from those resting hands.

But the inherent will-power which had propped up Widow Borden beside uncountable washtubs, now enabled Anne to carry on. It masked her dark-hued face in inscrutableness. It laid low the clinging longing for the old life of ease and—yes—splendor. It aided her to learn the art of simple every day washing and baking and sewing. And of course it didn't take much of a wrench to unloose her little store in knowledge of music and languages and the preparation of a chafing-dish feast. Yet the sobs which she stifled of nights against her pillow and the ache in her heart which grew and grew until it lessened under its own weight, seemed a needless, heartless price to pay for a comfortable ride in a fine upholstered perambulator. But Life is Life, and youth is youth.

Anne kept tenacious hold unto Life's skirts even after her tumble. And more to be commended she held tightly to her ladyhood, that attainment so easily acquired and as easily lost. Something in a way, so startling that it attracted the attention of Mrs. Lewis-Osborne, Anne's mistress.

That august lady was often wont to declare over her luncheon, at tea, and even while dining out; whenever the servant-problem was discussed:

"Oh, my servants—la—la," then with a gush of very pleasing laughter—"but I have one jewel—my nurse-maid—with me four years this June; as straight as a string and every move a lady; why her poise is wonderful and she carries her head high, like a queen. My Dicky-boy's manners are due to her and I intend to hold her by all means for the sake of Elizabeth." Then with the manner of one handing out a rare tid-bit, in lowered tones: "It's odd, too, she's colored." And always that information was followed by a grand chorus, "Oh, you don't say, colored."

There came a summer, when Anne went to the coast with the Lewis-Osbornes, to a little town, which she thought was the prettiest spot in all the world; where mountains and valley and ocean suffused their beauty in a matchless rivalry; where the purple mountains misted and shaded through a thousand hues into the green of valley, while the valley's green caught the gold of sun and silver of moon's and merged tremblingly into the green of ocean. And Life so wondrously kind when she chooses, followed Anne over the mountains and down through the valley, on by the sea.

A high rock wall surrounded the premises of the Lewis-Osbornes. A high rock wall that shut in an old-fashioned garden, a sundial and many rustic seats and a musical fountain—and here it was that Anne spent the mornings with her charges. She always sang for the children, and here singing was easy, the thing to be done amid flowers and a tinkling fountain. Whenever their dusky nurse-maid sang the children left their play to draw close, listening with the wonder and appreciation of childhood.

All unknowing, Anne had another listener. Big Jim Moore, the neighborhood gardener; a genius in his line. A wonderful sight to see, great bronze giant that he was, handling flowers with the exquisite finesse of a master. Any artist, who knew his business enough to depict feeling, soul, or art, or whatever you call it, and expert enough. To catch that great black fellow with his brawny arms bared as his great hands played lovingly over a rosebush, while more or less little children tugged at his garments as he was to be seen any summer morning would make a canvass fit to be placed side by side with any of the great Shepherd and Lamb paintings and its significance would be by far the greater.

One morning, so sunny a morning until the sky had a golden sheen, Anne sang and the little ones stopped their play to listen—on the other side of the wall Jim Moore stopped his work to listen. And Life draped in rosy garments danced around and about giving ear to the song, she sang:

> I feel the sap to the bough returning,
> I knew the skylarks' transport fine;
> I feel the fountains' wayward yearning,
> I love and the world is mine.

Jim Moore listened until he caught the refrain, then roguishly chimed in with a deep-throated whistle. And the singing and the whistling combined faultlessly and sweetly and continued so until the song was done.

With one accord Anne and the children stood up.

"Let's climb the wall and see," cried the elder.

"Oh, do; oh, do," piped the younger.

Without a word, Anne swung across the garden, the children in hot pursuit. A moment and the wall was scaled. A moment and Anne Borden looked down deep, deep into the gentle eyes of big Jim Moore.

"It's you." They exclaimed simultaneously, as though this their first meeting was but the renewal of an age-long friendship.

Ah, Life, what a woman you are, with all your capriciousness and derisiveness and your jokes which you sometimes take too far, yet do you ever pause to bow in obeisance to youth and love such as this clasping of hands to follow after you.

Competitor 2 (Aug.–Sept. 1920): 105–108.

The Hand That Fed

THE INSTANT IT WAS TRULY KNOWN that Aunt Mina had taken "in" "poor white-trash," hauteur and contempt was the old woman's portion. Damning her beyond any leniency, to their minds, was the fact that Sam Wilkins and the entire Truelove family and Joe Thomson, went in a body to warn her, giving her specific instances, their own personal experiences, of dire calamities which befell black folk for harboring "poor white-trash."

Remember old man Bruce, they told her. Hadn't he taken "in" a whole family, fed them, clothed them, and sheltered them like a father. Then, surely Aunt Mina had not forgotten, how in the early hours of morning, the hour when old Bruce arose to milk his cherished cow, the white woman alarmed the neighborhood with her shrill screams for help. Who of them could ever forget it? How old Bruce was horribly put to death and his little holdings of land and his pigs and his mule and his chickens, even his beloved cow, confiscated by the "white-trash" he had befriended.

Then, too, her neighbors thought in this wise: In this day and time, Negroes no longer had cause to subserve and cringe before white folk. It smacked entirely of antebellum days for black folk to look after "whites" merely because the latter were white. It was a truth undeniable, that let a "white" be down and out and he would seek to come up on the back of blacks. But little by little the "black" was beginning to think, "if a white is in need let him take himself off to his own kith and kin." Little by little the "black" was growing tired of practicing the age-old rule of humility: "If thy neighbor smite thee on thy left cheek turn the other unto him also." They had done just that and in consequence their jawbones were well nigh threadbare from many untold smitings. They were seeking something else now, without any desire to meet spite with spite or malice with malice; they were seeking to make themselves immune from receiving evil for good. Hourly they grew wary of laying themselves liable to receiving a dose of this—the bitterest of pills—ingratitude.

Nevertheless, Aunt Mina, despite all they had to say, gave shelter and food and raiment to Myra Stellwell and her child. She opened the door, not alone to her neat little cottage, but to her friendly heart as well, to this woman and her little one, derelicts, of an alien race.

Myra Stellwell was not quite an adventuress—she was too dilatory and unprogressive for that, but she possessed the main essential for being one; she was unutterably selfish. All her life, she had been a drifter, a bit of useless flotsam. Born of a tight-rope walker and a devil-of-a-fellow whose stunt was climbing the spiral tower upon a sphere; she grew up to young womanhood with the stench of wild animals and filthy sawdust and sweltering humanity in her nostrils. Then having remained long enough to imbibe all the ugliness of her surroundings, she eloped, if such is possible from a third-rate traveling show; with a shiftless vagabond, who had lately attached himself to their equipage.

Their consort was a miserable failure—an occurrence that was a crime; when it brought forth another precious life to imbibe the filth and passion of two worthless beings. Six months after her child's coming, Myra Stellwell was adrift once more, yet even her vagrant soul was momentarily stirred by her babe's dependence. And with slovent efforts to do for the child, she slopped about in one restaurant after another as waitress or dishwasher, until discharged for inefficiency or dishonesty.

If unusually hard-pressed, she resorted to charity, ofttimes receiving substantial assistance. But the restlessness of her spirit kept her ever moving from the harum-scarum catch-as-catch-can existence in the larger cities to the opulent charitableness obtained from the pitying credulous of the smaller towns, then on again. Thus had been her career for the three and half years since the coming of her little girl, Eloise.

Myra Stellwell arrived in Overvale in the fall. Employing her usual tricks, she worked at the town's two restaurants and was discharged from one for slovenness, from the other for theft. For a short while, she performed in Overvale's one hotel as chambermaid and as thoroughly disgusted the proprietor with her sickening flirtations, he turned her off within the week. A kindhearted woman, whose sympathy was aroused because of the child, befriended her, giving Myra board and lodgings for herself and child in pay for a few household tasks; but upon finding that Myra simply would not do, quite unfeelingly turned her out one evening just at dusk, in the dead of winter. In Overvale the winters are severe.

Then it was, that Myra made her way southward, following the main thoroughfare, leading across the tracks into Overvale's Negro settlement. There were stores and restaurants and also a hotel owned by the blacks. And there were many warm, snug-looking cottages nestling in neat clean yards, in every direction Myra looked. She made a quick mental survey of those she saw, aided by the street lights, and decided to try her luck at the pretty little brown house to her right, well on towards the end of the street.

It was old Mina Goodwin's home. A woman beloved by all who knew her, a steadfast reliable creature, as swarthy as a jet bead, kindhearted and credulous. A woman who had performed nobly and well; eleven children had suckled her breast, and she had worked shoulder to shoulder with her man for their upkeeping. They had been schooled and taught how to make honest livings and they had taken unto themselves mates and gone off to live their own lives, not wholly forgetful, to be sure, of their old widowed mother; but to say the least, very unmindful of her. Of them all, Aunt Mina was able to lay her toil-worn old hand on just one of them—a son, Daniel—who lived twenty miles away, down country on his own little farm.

He was a good son. He sent her fruits and vegetables in season and plump fat hens for her Sunday's dinners.

Aunt Mina never confessed it but she was lonely. What woman is not, who has mothered a brood of noisy lusty children and then, suddenly finds herself, childless, alone, living in silent empty rooms day in and day out. She had taken to muttering to herself long winter evenings, as she sat alone by her fire in a little old low armless rocker, swaying back and forth, back and forth, watching the embers flare and glow and darken into ashes against the sagging grate of her little heater.

Aunt Mina was enjoying the evening thus, when Myra Stellwell rapped on her door; the unexpected sound jerked the old woman into startled alertness. The little old rocker thumped its surprise as it came to an abrupt halt. The knock puzzled Aunt Mina. No, none of her neighbors were ill, it was not that and it was too late for any neighborly borrowing of sugar or coffee for next morning's early meal.

Then Myra rapped again, imperatively, the manner most suited to her selfish nature, bringing Aunt Mina's surmising to an end. Aunt Mina arose and scuttled to her door, unbarred it and opened it wide.

To kind old eyes like Aunt Mina's, the sight of a bedraggled woman and a little child, shelterless on a bitter winter's night, was heart rending. At the moment she thought not on the color of the woman and child before her, of nothing, save that they were pitiable human beings in need of warmth and shelter and unhesitatingly, she bid them enter.

Myra stepped in instantly and as if it was hers by divine right, made straight for the little old comfortable rocker in its coziest nook by the fire, and sat down quite unbidden. The little girl, a frail little thing, huddled against Myra's knee.

Aunt Mina, who had been occupied fastening the door, came and put more fuel into the heater. Before any words were spoken, she disappeared to return with an old pair of carpet slippers and some of her own warm stockings for Myra's wet and sodden feet. After fidgeting here and there after the fashion of the very aged, bringing this and that to contribute to her guests comfort, she placed another chair near the fire and sat down.

Myra had pushed the little girl to one side and was busily exchanging her shoes. Aunt Mina lifted the child into her lap. The little one contentedly pressed her curly head against the ample curve of the old woman's bosom and fell asleep.

Meanwhile, Myra contentedly at ease, affected timid embarrassment and in a voice that quavered and broke on bravely checked tears—(Myra could certainly act)—told her kindhearted listener the ups and downs of her life. Barring an account of the part her own selfish, shiftless, slothful self had played in the shaping of her existence, Myra told mostly the truth. Her career had been quite full of pitfalls and her feet had treaded enough mire holes to make any life miserable. Yet on the whole, Myra thought nothing at all about her previous hardships and no phase of life had been too low to repulse her; but her recital left one to suppose she had fought and struggled valorously to surmount every evil; and though, now beaten, in the sense that she was reduced to utter poverty, helpless, and at the mercy of strangers, she was still unbeaten, in the sense that she was pure and clean-hearted—a wholesome woman.

The outcome was: Myra and the child remained with Aunt Mina. In the beginning, it was very much like having two cherished guests added to her household. Aunt Mina cooked in her good old-fashioned way, meals, which seemed to Myra veritable feasts, although bought from the store—the one around the corner that adjoined her own property, and owned by a white man. She felt that she should have gone on further to Handy & Son, shopkeepers of her own race, but this little place was so near and her old bones were not as supple as they once had been, and, too, this shop carried just such things as she now saw fit to purchase—stuffed olives, bottled cherries, scarlet pimientos, and little pots of marmalades wrapped around with foreign labels, dainty tins of potted ham and pickled tongue, curved jars of salad oils and sauces, and small flat cans of delicious fish still swimming life-like in a thick and golden liquid. For Myra relished things of this sort so.

And indeed she did. In the first few months of her sojourn with old Aunt Mina, "she ate like a hog" and plumped out as surprisingly as though someone had inserted an air-pump into her body.

The little girl grew sturdier and rosy also, but unlike her mother, she repaid the old black woman full measure, giving her the sweetest tribute on earth, a child's unstinted worship.

Myra even took advantage of this, by leaving the little girl to Aunt Mina's care almost entirely. Caring for the child had always been burdensome to Myra and she was not one to let such a chance to shirk the responsibility slip away.

Aunt Mina's bill at the little shop around the corner began to mount with the passing of each month. Compared to its usual economical rating it was enormous—it became startling. And Aunt Mina had to sell several of the fat plump hens, which came up from her son's little farm, to help round out the sums.

All the same, Myra lounged about in the old woman's rooms and considered certain things to herself. At such times, her glassy green eyes took on a brilliant glitter, like a cunning reptile, for in her heart she coveted with a bitter envy, Aunt Mina's simple possessions. Often, when the old woman had taken little Eloise by the hand and gone on one of her numerous little trips to the store around the corner, Myra would stand up with clenched fists and tight-shut teeth through which she spat out horrible imprecations upon the old black woman. "How dare she, how dare she, have all this and I have noth-

ing." Her malevolent envy was frightful to see. Then she began at the
end of the third month to plan and act.

"Auntie," she said one day, in her sweetest manner, "Let me run
things awhile, cook, you know, and do the shopping. I'm just tired to
death lying about doing nothing."

"Lawsy, child," exclaimed Aunt Mina, "you'll do no such thing."
But on seeing Myra's assimilated crestfallen air, she went on, "though
you could run out and do the buying, 't would save me a mighty heap
o' steps."

Myra gave vent to effusive delight, then turned away to hide her
crafty smile. Old Aunt Mina, who was beating a cake, began to sing
as unsuspecting as the fly who walked into the spider's parlor.

The very next morning, Myra went to the little store around the
corner. Her third or fourth visit there placed her on a free familiar
footing with the evil-visaged white proprietor. He made most of his
profit by overcharging for his line of fancy articles and not by any too
flourishing trade, so the pair had many an idle moment to dawdle
away, with Myra perched carelessly upon the counter, her feet swing-
ing and the shopkeeper lolling beside her.

"Say, what's yer game, camping with that old nigger-woman?" he
queried one day.

"Game," cried Myra. "Game!" She looked him straight in the eye
with her green glassy orbs like pin-points. She read him unerringly,
then she answered slowly and distinctly with a little pause after each
of her words:

"I'll be sole owner of that old nigger-woman's little brown bungalow inside the year—that's my game."

"S-a-a-ay," ejaculated the shopkeeper, "you're sure's some gal."

Aunt Mina had given up her own warm bedchamber to Myra. The
constant caring for two others had depleted her little store of dollars, so she was forced to do without many of the necessities to
which she was accustomed and such privations at her age was merely
an invitation to illness. Consequently, when the winter, an unusually

90 || Unfinished Masterpiece

severe one, commenced to break, the old woman was taken with la-grippe. She was a very sick old woman.

Myra, her opportunity at hand, ran things presumptuously. The ill-visaged shopkeeper—Myra and he were great friends now—supplied the money for her heartless crafty scheme. With this, she paid the doctor and the druggist, afterwards making out fraudulent bills with herself as creditor and of course old Aunt Mina the debtor. The account at the store around the corner was made to climb up amazingly, while all the little minor expenses of a household were doubled and trebled under Myra's regime. In truth, as far as figures went—and in the white man's old familiar vernacular, "What's in white and black can't lie"—Old Aunt Mina owed Myra Stellwell a snug little sum at the end of her two months illness.

Then, too, the illness left Aunt Mina's perceptions clouded. She came forth from her bleak little bed-room, a dazed and somewhat blundering old woman. And Myra made the most of it assuming control of all Aunt Mina's affairs quite arrogantly.

During this period, the old woman and the little child were inseparable. The former was yet pathetically content puttering about out-of-doors, tending the few remaining plump hens that had come from her son's little farm. When there was nothing more to be done for her fowls, she sat on an old bench under a gnarled plum tree and muttered to herself. Often little Eloise, always near by, would pause in her play to ask, "What you talking about, Auntie?" To which the old woman would reply, "Never mind, honey, never you mind."

There came the day when Myra confronted the old woman, accusingly:

"I say, old woman," she cried insultingly, "it's high time you set about paying some of your debts—the debts you owe me—me."

Aunt Mina was dumbfounded: she sat down helplessly on the edge of a chair and gasped:

"Debts—you—I—owe—you?"

"Yes, me!" cried Myra, working herself into a fury. "Me," she screamed crazily. "If you want proof, I'll get it." So saying, she flew out of the door down the street, around the corner to the grocer's and was back accompanied by the ill-visaged shopkeeper before Aunt Mina had fully recovered her breath.

The shopkeeper's manner was suavely considerate, a wide contrast to Myra's impetuous fury, and Aunt Mina was entirely taken in by his smooth pleasant demeanor. She turned towards him imploringly, beseeching him to explain things.

The crafty fellow drew a chair close alongside the old woman's and sat down, then he took from the inner pocket of his coat, a folder and began to produce bill after bill—bills for groceries, bills for fuel, bills revealing item after item of nothing save chicken-feed—a half dozen old hens, greedy fowls, the amount of food they had consumed.

"You see, my dear woman," said the shopkeeper; when he finally reached the end of the accounts, "You see, you never would have been able to swim out, if it hadn't been for that kindhearted creature yonder"—he jerked a huge and dirty thumb towards Myra, who stood all ablaze at the end of the room—"and its only natural, why it stands to reason, now that you are all fit and able to be up and about, that she should want some of her money back. You were a mighty sick woman, Auntie, and all alone here, you'd been forced to have a nurse or a'gone to a hospital—Well, you didn't have to do either. That kindhearted creature yonder"—he gesticulated again with his big dirty thumb towards Myra; who had now, slackened some of her display of anger and resorted to tears.

The old black woman thrust out earnestly—"yes, yes, I am grateful to Miss Myra for all she done for me—and if she'll only wait, I'll pay her every cent she charged for nursing and caring for me. Those other bills, the doctors and yours and all the rest, you all know me, you'll wait—you'll carry that along till I get straight."

"But my dear woman," broke in the shopkeeper, "you don't seem to understand. Miss Myra bore all those expenses—she's paid those bills long and a-merry ago out of her own pocket, thinking it would be easier for you to just pay everything to her—her being right here with you and all, she banked on you being fair, never looked for all this from one she'd befriended—no sir."

"I never told her to—I never—" groaned the old woman gazing at Myra uncomprehendingly. Then with a flash of her old quick intuition, she flung out: "How could she—how could she—when she never had a penny, nary a penny of her own all the time she been here?"

"Tut—tut," said the shopkeeper suavely, "how could you know that? A white woman's business is her own."

Aunt Mina scarcely heard him. Her eyes were riveted upon Myra, whose anger had revived at Aunt Mina's feeble protest.

She flung out her arms in unbelieving frenzy, screaming, "That woman owes me the roof over her old wooly head. You do, you do, you hideous old black witch. Go! Go! Go! Or I'll put you out; I'll put you out."

"I think," said the shopkeeper softly, suavely, but with a flint-like quality to his tones, "you had best clear out—here's the proof—" he tapped the folder with his pencil, "proof enough to hang you, it's all her against you. Let me tell you, old woman, you are in debt, a bad thing anyhow, and the best that can be done right now is to turn over this here little place of your'n, not much, doesn't half cover the sum you owe, but—"

"My home, my home," moaned the old black woman and for an instant her old head fell forward as though lifeless upon her chest, then she arose wearily and went out.

She entered the little bleak room that had been hers since Myra's arrival and folded a few old faded garments into an old-fashioned satchel. She had in mind her son Daniel's farm twenty miles down country. She had no money. Though a sale of her six plump hens would have netted her enough to reach her destination with a dribble of change remaining, but it would be useless to argue over their possession.

She went out of the house—out of the gate, on down the street, quite resolutely; but her heart in her bosom was heavy, heavy as stone; now and again, it lurched painfully, and the old woman pressed her hand to her side, while a curious bewildered look passed over her face. She trudged on, and at sundown she had reached the outskirts of town. And still she pressed on, doggedly.

She had come to a bit of woodland; when she paused to listen, because she thought she heard her name called. She had halted her steps several times before for the same reason. She looked back over the way she had come, but her bleared old eyes could discern no one. She started onwards. Then she heard her name yet more distinctly. She recognized the voice of little Eloise. She began retracing her steps swiftly, precipitately, and turning a curve in the road where the woods was thinnest, she saw the golden-haired child plodding wearily, sobbingly towards her.

The old black woman's heart seemed now no longer a stone; but a throbbing pain-racked thing that strained to bursting at this evidence of a child's unstinted love. It quivered and lurched and her black face ashened with pain, yet she flung herself onward with old arms outstretched and happy tears blinding her vision.

When the child was reached, the old woman's ebbing strength revived and she stooped and gathered the little one into her arms, hugging her tightly to her breast. She went on, thus, a short way, a very short way, then she was forced to sit down to rest. Little Eloise cuddled beside her.

"Ello wouldn't let her auntie run away. She run 'way, too—Ello run 'way, too," she said before she fell asleep in the curve of Aunt Mina's encircling arms.

The old woman leaned against a tree trunk for support. Her eyes were heavy. She wanted to sleep. But she could not sleep, she must keep awake to watch for those who would surely come in pursuit of the child. Oh, dear Lord, but she was sleepy—so sleepy. Queer things flashed in and out of her mind. What was it? Which one of her children used to read to her from the Bible? Yes, yes, of course, little Lilly, her girl Lilly; who had married and gone so far away. How did it go? Oh, how in the world did it go—that passage about—that about: "COME UNTO ME"—No—yes—that was it, "AND I WILL GIVE YOU REST." And REST that was to sleep, just to sleep, but no—no—no, she must not sleep, not yet, she had to keep awake, soon they would come for the little one—she must keep watch—for the sake of her beloved—. They would find her too; but she did not care, they could no longer harm her. She was falling to sleep and someone was singing, "COME UNTO ME YE WHO ARE WEARY AND I WILL GIVE YOU REST."

Was someone really singing, her eyes stared wide to see, was someone truly singing or was it whispered in the treetops overhead and in the grasses at her feet? How could anyone care for things like little brown houses that had been home and ungrateful folks that bit the hand that fed, when wonderful sweet voices repeated over and over soothing, comforting words like those—"COME UNTO ME."

Finally her heart gave one more painful breath-taking lurch and the curious bewildered look that overspread her countenance, faded into one of great content giving her swarthy wrinkled kind old face a strangely unfamiliar look—for she had fallen to sleep.

Competitor 2 (Dec. 1920): 259–261, 293, 295.

The Little Grey House

IT WAS BUILT OF CEMENT, of a lighter hue than most cement houses, so it was dubbed the little grey house.

Somehow, its builders pervaded every inch of its rough exterior with an inviting air. Even before it was finished—and we all know most incomplete houses are so mussy and dreary with daubs of paint and spattered lime and splotches of mud and shavings and blocks of wood and the workmen's tools lying all about—but this was different.

The unfinished windows suggested gauzy curtains and flowering plants. The littered interior with its yawning doorways revealing other unplastered chambers and yet more clutter, gave a cheery promise of clean-swept, cozy rooms. The little squat chimney that lifted its stubby nose into the air from the left-hand corner of its roof hinted with all its might, of the hearth-fire that would soon cast its rosy warmth over the inmates of the little grey house; while the chimney that poked its nose towards the sky at the rear of the roof, was a silent witness of many smokes it would exhale from the cooking of savory meals.

Timothy passed the little grey house every morning on his way to work and every evening on his way home—

home to his untidy bachelor apartment, where he, himself, made the bed and cooked the meals and washed the dishes whenever they were washed, that was, when Timothy found his cupboard shelves were bare and his sink over-filled with plates and cups.

He was interested from the first—from the moment he saw the men laying off the site for the little grey house. Every evening he paused to take in what had been accomplished during the day. He inspected the foundation—noted the number of rooms there were to be—guessed boyishly just which would be the bed-room, living-room, and kitchen. He hoped heartily there would be an honest-to-goodness kitchen and none of your new-fangled, fool-notion kitchenettes.

"Even if they eat in the kitchen 'twill be better'n one of those fool kitchenettes," he soliloquized. "For now, what in heck is a home without a kitchen, if 'taint just like a ship without a rudder I'll be blowed." He passed on, his broad good-natured face wreathed in smiles at his own wit.

The little grey house was nearing completion when it happened the first time. At the next street crossing he met her. He remembered that she was just about to take the step up to the sidewalk.

Hillsvale was such an up and down hill little place—that each walk began or ended in a flight of steps—and he had politely stood aside to let her ascend.

She acknowledged the little courtesy with the tiniest scantiest acknowledgment that could be.

Friendly Timothy was made somewhat crestfallen by her chilly manner, wondered if it was just her scant politeness or more of his "infernal, confounded knack at getting in bad with the ladies."

Leastways the encounter put an end to that day's pleasant musing about the little grey house. It made the boiled and steaming "hot-dogs" and the loaf of home-made bread still warm from the oven, that kind old Mrs. Bloomsay had given him for his supper, and the butter and the tea and the cabbage, he had prepared so painstakingly that morning, guided by a vivid memory of his mother's cold-slaw into a semblance of that dish, and the baker's blue-berry pie, which he meant to use as the climax of his evening's meal taste, as he said, "Like gol-darned saw-dust in his mouth."

"The truth is," he flayed himself further in comical petulance, "you are plumb put out because a cross old hen gave you the icy stare. Oh boy, she's got your goat."

He tried reading his evening's paper and found himself glaring menacingly at the front page whereon in great black type announced the sweeping victory of a political candidate, who was especially distasteful to him; he flung the paper from him disgustedly.

He tried smoking, but his cigar—one of the same brand he smoked invariably—was the rankest, vilest weed he ever put in his mouth. It was tossed vehemently into the fire.

He stood up then in the middle of his mussy kitchen and scowled at the littered supper-table and the sink full of dirty dishes, then suddenly rolled up his sleeves and gave battle to the disorder until everything shone tidy and neat. "Be blowed," he said and smiled, almost restored to his usual good nature, "if it don't look like a woman did it." But there . . . he had spoken the unlucky word . . . woman. As he uttered it, his thoughts reverted to the object of that species who was causing all the trouble.

"Who in the deuce is she anyhow?" he exclaimed wrathfully. . . . As there was no one to answer him, he presently went to bed, with a conscience as clean as any man's could be, who had lived forty years in this sin-filled world—re-enforced with a kindly good-nature, and a body keyed to the fatigue point by a fun day of hard work soon brought refreshing sleep, accompanied by a dream, which, he remembered vaguely, featured a plump little brown woman with a regular apple-dumpling sort of a face. For Timothy was certain that an apple-dumpling browned to a turn, and spiced and sugared to suit an epicure's appetite, was the neatest description for the little woman's soft full cheeks and rounded chin.

Altogether he was pleased with that face; until he remembered the eyes. "My stars," he would say, "some ice! Oh boy!" Only, he recalled through the indistinctness of his dream, those eyes had been soft and tender and he declared wonderingly, as he kicked off the covers and rolled out of bed next morning, "They got his goat."

With another day's work "neatly put over" and the makings of a nifty meal—a juicy steak, a package of potato-chips, a dozen freshly baked rolls all tucked into the curve of his arm; with nothing in the world to worry about; the incident of the evening before almost swept from his mind—Timothy paused almost from habit before the little grey house.

"I'll be blowed, if you ain't the prettiest little box of a house I've seen yet!"

Then beset with the thoughts of his yet-to-be-cooked steak, he hurried on—and there—almost in the same spot approached the woman. Timothy grinned broadly over the coincident and just as he had done the previous evening stood aside politely as she ascended. And again just to a T she acknowledged the little courtesy with the tiniest, scantiest acknowledgment, so scant, that only an intent—a very intent observer could have discerned it at all.

"Well, one thing's certain, old girl," thought Timothy, "you're sure no killer for looks. I reckon it's the old girl's way of pulling off the high and mighty that's got my goat. Anyhow," he announced quite spiritedly to himself, "I'll be blowed if I don't fry this steak and eat every scrap of it—old haughty one, you're not going to spoil my eats every single night, not on your life."

"I wonder," mused Opal Kent half angrily, who all unknowingly lived in Timothy's mind as the plump little lady with the apple-dumpling face, "who on earth that grinning Jacob of a man can be?"

Opal Kent had never received any marked attention from men, so Timothy's eager politeness was bewildering to her simple soul; and his broad smile, which she so contemptuously termed a grin, exasperated her to the limit and what made it worse, she could not reason why—and his intent scrutiny of her as she passed—it was maddening.

"The horrid, horrid thing!" she exclaimed aloud, then in an undertone which sounded cooingly soft as it wafted away on the breeze:

"But he isn't bad-looking a bit, not a bit."

Opal Kent was one of the jolliest, dearest little women in the world, good-hearted to a fault and responsive as a kitten to kindness and gentle treatment; but at present, she was all out of sorts. She was lonely and homesick—homesick as only a homeless woman can be and she was disheartened. Here she was already past the thirty-mile sign in years, and as Timothy himself had concluded, "In no way a killer for looks." All in the world she could do was cook and keep house. Of course, there was her crocheting and tatting and knitting, but no valuation could be put upon that, thought Opal, for where in the world could you find a homely old spinster fond of her hearthfire who couldn't?

Poor lonely Opal; like all disheartened people she belittled her attainments, for her cooking was sheerest witchery and she belonged to those rare women who could, given the stimulation of having near her, those she loved, could convert a bare spot in a desert into a home.

To be sure, of this last attribute, none save old Joseph Kent could testify and since he had died a year ago, his testimony was hopelessly out of the question.

Opal had always kept house for her father. As far back as she could remember she had been the little woman of his household. A distant relative had helped old Joseph raise her to an early age of independence and since then, she had been the little mistress of their home.

"Old Joe Kent" had been a grim, forbidding old man, who repulsed rather than encouraged any friendships for himself and daughter. They had lived a bleak and lonely life, relieved only by the love they bore each other.

Old Kent had uncanny success with his pigs and chickens and by supplying his neighbors' tables with these commodities, earned a livelihood. He looked forward a bit for Opal's sake and insured himself quite heavily and the payment of those premiums had eaten the heart out of his meager income.

Opal had stinted and economized for every dress and every hat or ribbon she had ever possessed. So plus her cooking and house-keeping was an almost instinctive frugality that saved seemingly val-ueless things and cunningly contrived them into articles of value. She made cunning baby shoes from a man's old, cast-off hat. She saved the vinegar off the pickles to mix her salad dressings, saved turkey feathers and made her own feather dusters, could take a nearly clean-picked chicken carcass, a grain or two of rice, a cabbage leaf, a cel-ery stalk and turn out soup with a savory odor that lingered in your nostrils for a fortnight and a pleasing taste that tickled your palate whenever you recalled it.

Almost simultaneously, with the sad occurrence of her father's death and the coming of the insurance money, old Judge Crowley prepared to move West for his wife's health. And Opal was prevailed upon to accompany them as cook.

"Why not?" reasoned Opal, for who in her little home town cared if she went or remained? It was enough to make one sour to think about it, for no one ever suspected how much Opal Kent longed for friendship and there was none among all her life-long acquaintances who could be called friend.

If someone had suggested to Opal that it was her father's fault, she would have been appalled. She would have repudiated it with every ounce of strength of her being. Her father, her dear, old, kind, indulgent dad! How she missed him! She could see him just as he used to be and it was sweet to remember how the lines of care faded from his face as he sat and watched her bustle about preparing the supper. His favorite place was beside the kitchen door, which faced westward. He always sat full in the golden shaft of sunlight. "It warms like nothing else on earth," had been his phrase. And Opal had come to time the evening meal with the fading of the sunlight from the door. Such had been their life together, replete with the nameless love tokens each had performed for the other, with no word of explanation to add to or distract their pleasure. "You are like your ma, girl," had been his one form of endearment, and she perceived that those six words summed up the strength of a love that had lasted unto death and beyond the grave and lived again in all of its wondrous beauty for herself.

The Crowleys had settled in Hillsvale six months ago and Opal Kent suddenly decided to invest her insurance money in a home. Hillsvale would be as good a place as any in which to spend her life, since she had no friends or any tie to bind her elsewhere. And forthwith, she had bought the lots and had the little grey house built.

She would rent it at first, of course, and work on, saving every cent of her money until she had enough to allow her to become mistress of the little grey house in earnest.

Then she would raise chickens. Just supposing, if she had fifty hens and got fifty eggs a day, as the ads in the farm papers guaranteed was the simplest thing to do . . . and she would keep bees, the Government bulletins extolled their virtue to the highest . . . a pleasant and profitable industry . . . and she would have a few bunnies, another profitable and little known money-maker, she wouldn't go into that so deeply, but a few would add variety to her meat supply, providing she could kill and eat them after fondling them, as she knew she would do. They were such cunning creatures with their pink noses forever wiggling and their bright eyes constantly watchful. She would have a nice old tabby cat and a collie pup and maybe after she was known in Hillsvale, little children would come to see her and her pets. She would keep a well-filled cookie jar, and of course there would be honey, and perhaps, oh perhaps, she would be ever and ever so happy as mistress of the little grey house, even though she was alone and friendless and had nothing, nothing, with which to challenge the coming lonely years. She was unable to suppress the shudder which came when she thought of that.

Taken from all angles, it is quite true that folks are the masters of their own destiny: only one must admit that catching hold of your own particular bit of destiny is nearly as futile a performance as a kitten swirling around trying to catch his tail. At least it appeared so to Opal all bolstered up with expectations over the little grey house.

The big "FOR RENT" sign which was tacked upon the little grey house as soon as it was finished failed to attract any notice whatever. It seemed that all the house hunters and all the disgruntled renters for once in their lives were happily settled and satisfied. Nobody rented Opal Kent's little place, by no means as soon as she expected and certainly not as soon as she had need for it to be.

The Crowleys, without any hint of their intentions, decided to move elsewhere. Opal, finding herself indefinitely linked to Hillsvale because of the little grey house, could not be induced to move with them.

Opal found another place and though it saved her from becoming stranded in a strange town, she did not like it. Not having learned how, she did not make friends readily and her work was confining, so she became acquainted with no one.

She was timid and self-conscious and oppressed by an overgrowing dread of loneliness, and like most homeless women, she was afraid, just afraid of everything. "Suppose," ran her thoughts, "I should lose my health, what then? Suppose I do not save enough before I am old. . . ."

She grew more and more reticent and her plump, round face grew overcast with dread and her eyes grew sharp. She watched people, watched the expression of their faces and construed them to portend queer things concerning herself, when for the most part her dumpty little figure passed among the crowds unnoticed. She wondered over Timothy's good-natured smile. "Why does he laugh at me so? Oh, dear, I must be funny, and, oh . . . oh, queer."

The first time Timothy saw the "FOR RENT" sign he stopped and gazed at it incredulously. "Well now," he said, "what nut built a house like that to rent? I was as sure as pop that it was going to be somebody's home—somebody who'd love every inch of it and take care of it and plant flowers around it, and all such as that. Now look at that there sign, 'FOR RENT'; just spoils the whole thing, be blowed if it don't."

He continued to meet Opal. In fact, his interest was divided between the little grey house and these meetings with the plump little woman. Taken together, they afforded Timothy something pleasant with which to wind up his lonely evenings. He would think of the little grey house and wonder who'd rent it, and he would think about the little woman, wondering who she was. No one he questioned seemed to know. At bed time he would turn in and maybe dream that he was Lord and Master of both the little woman and the little grey house.

Then as unexpected as the "FOR RENT" sign had been was the "FOR SALE" sign which Timothy glanced up to see one evening as he passed. In smaller lettering the placard stated, further information secured from PITMAN'S REALTY COMPANY.

It set Timothy to thinking. He was preoccupied when he passed the little dumpty woman. So for once Opal failed to see him grinning, but with a woman's inconsistence, she found herself wondering what in the world had happened to chase his smiles away.

And if Timothy had not been so absorbed he would have been sure to notice the traces of tears which lingered in the little woman's eyes.

Opal was on her way to the little grey house. She had enjoyed so much to go there when her hopes were high. She had found grim satisfaction in seeing it after she knew that as a business venture it was a hopeless failure. And now, that she had decided to sell it, from necessity, she found a torturing delight in looking upon it.

Yes, the place she had was unendurable. She couldn't stand the contempt and the rude treatment, the family for whom she now worked, seemed to think was a cook's portion. She would sell the little place and get out of it whatever she could and write the Crowleys that she would join them.

That night, Timothy made up his mind. "Be blowed, if I won't buy it myself. . . ." 'Twas a shame for a house like that to go to waste!

"Who knows?" he questioned, "I might find me a wife, and even if I don't, 'cause a man's single is no sign he has to live like a pig. Gosh no! I'll set out a lilac bush and some flowers and plant some trees. Anyhow, I'll buy the dinged little place and get it off my mind."

Two days later, Opal Kent went to the realty office and transacted her portion of the business pertaining to the sale of the little grey house. She received her money—nearly as much as the little grey house had cost—minus the commission.

With the money in her possession, her plans changed again. She would stay in Hillsvale and see who had purchased the little grey house.

Timothy Martin stopped that evening to inspect his property thoroughly. He went from room to room, there were five, a nice spacious kitchen with built-in cupboards and cabinets, and one end which made an alcove built almost entirely of glass, a stationary table and chairs stood resplendent, invitingly coaxing one to eat. "Holy Pete!" ejaculated Timothy, "I'll plant honeysuckle to climb all over that there glass . . . and won't it be pretty?" In the other rooms, he found window seats with hinged covers and more built-in cabinets and book cases. "Gosh," he exclaimed, "mighty pretty, but it's just been built for a woman. A woman's the only creature on earth that can care for this sort of trick."

He was nearly through with his round of inspection, when he stopped short, startled by a sound. "Gee," he muttered and listened. Again the sound came. "Be blowed, it sounds like someone crying." Timothy quietly retraced his steps, finding nothing until he entered the kitchen.

And there, in the waning sunlight which poured into the glass-walled alcove, beside the table, with her head bowed on her arms, sat the little woman, his plump little apple-dumpling woman, crying, just crying, thought Timothy, "like a great big baby."

Timothy stood stock still and watched her, watched her with a mingled delight and dismay and consternation; delight to find her there, dismay that she was crying and at the very end of his wits for fear his presence would frighten her away.

What should he do? Then a quivering little voice restored him to his senses.

"Oh, it's you—it's you! Did you buy it?"

Timothy sensed that she was speaking of the little grey house, and nodded his head in assent. Then in an eager desire to cheer her up, he began to talk in his cheery booming voice.

"Though, I'll be blowed, Miss, the blame little box was intended for a woman and not for the likes of me. All these here fixings tells you that. Now if I had a wife. . . . Say, now, you mustn't cry any more. Just you listen to me. I was saying that if I had a wife to put-ter around and fix this here trinket of a house like it ought to be fixed . . . I'd be the happiest man alive. Gee, Miss, I'm a demon when it comes to setting out vines and flowers and I'd have the yard out front looking like a bit of fairy land and we'd have chickens in the back and maybe a wee turnip patch."

"And," put in Opal, wholly unaware of the strangeness of it all, "I'd planned to have some bees too and just a handful of bunnies. Oh, don't you like to watch 'em wiggle their noses? . . . and I'd meant to have flowers too, holly-hocks and roses and lark-spurs growing everywhere, and a lilac bush under the bedroom window and hon-eysuckle and climbing roses over the ones in the dining room and I hadn't quite decided what I'd have over the windows in the living room, perhaps I'd have left 'em bare so's to look out and see folks passing . . ."

"Say you," burst in Timothy excitedly, "did you have this house built?" Thrust back into reality by his question, Opal could not speak, for tears choked back her words and her plump little shoulders heaved piteously.

In the wee interval in which he watched her second outburst, good-hearted, good-natured, forty-year-old bachelor, Timothy made a few swift calculations concerning his weeping companion. That in the main they were correct was not surprising for Timothy earned his livelihood by an ability to size up people. His heart jumped exultingly as he concluded she was not married and never had been. It clutched in pity, as he decided she wept thus because she was lonely and friendless and homeless, for he discerned from her tears that the little box of a house had been built to be her home. It took but a minute for his quick mind to ferret out this . . . then the blunt fashion that had ever been his custom that was the main spring of his "infernal, confounded knack of getting in bad with the ladies," expressed itself blurtingly . . .

"There . . . there . . . there," he punctuated each word with a bearish pat on Opal's heaving shoulder. "What in all heck, you crying about now, didn't I say I wanted a wife . . . ?"

And say what you will, the real mating among humans is like the birds, instinctive and unerring, for presently Opal's plumply rounded face was lifted to receive Timothy's smacking kiss; while the kindly sun, blinking his red-gold eye, like a jocose inebriate, slipped quietly away, out of the glass covered alcove, leaving them, master and mistress, in full possession of the little grey house.

Appeared in two parts: *Half-Century Magazine* 13 (July–Aug. 1922): 4, 17, 19; 13 (Sept.–Oct. 1922): 4, 21.

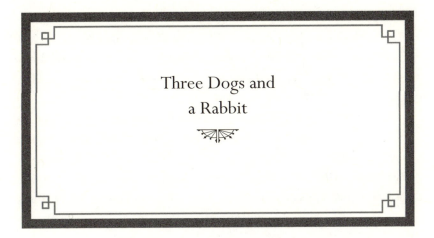

Three Dogs and a Rabbit

"THIS, THAT I'M ABOUT TO RELATE," said Timothy Phipps, "isn't much of a story, though, you might upon hearing it weave it into a ripping good yarn. I'm not much of a talker or writer. Now maybe when I'm in my cups or in the last stages of a delirious fever—I might attempt to—write." He tilted his head, with its fringe of rough grey hair, a bit backwards and sidewise and laughed. His laughter seeming to echo—write, write, write.

Tinkling with fine spirits and good humor, he ceased laughing to inquire roguishly: "What, say, are the ingredients of a story? A plot? Ah, yes, a plot. Ho! ho! ho! The only plot in this rigmarole, my dear fellow, is running, hard to catch, a sure enough running plot. Characters. To be sure we must have characters: A pretty girl, a brave hero, a villain and love. A setting. Of course there must be a setting, an atmosphere, a coloring. We'll say moonlight and a rippling brook and a night bird singing nocturnal hymns in a forest of love. Love pirouetting in the silvery moonlight, love splashing and singing in a rippling brook. Love trilling and fluting in a bird's song—Love and a pretty girl—Love and a brave hero—Love and a villain made penitent and contrite; because of love. Bye the bye, there is no living person who could not fancy the beginning, imagine the entanglements, conceive the climax, unfold the developments, reveal the solution and picture the finale, having such material at hand. But," laughed Timothy, "none such—none such in what I'm a-telling."

Shedding his joviality for a more serious mien, he queried—

"Have you ever thought how very few really lovely women one meets in a life time? Our pretty young debutantes are far too sophisticated; while our age-mellowed matrons affect *naiveté,* and our bustling housewives are too preoccupied with directing the destinies of nations to be attractive in the least.

"Men? Bother the men. We are but animals at best. Alert and crafty, lazy and jovial; just as chance decrees, and monotonously alike in our dependence upon woman. All of us are made or marred by our contacts with women. Whenever chance draws her draperies aside to allow a lovely woman to cross our path, it leaves an ineffaceable mark upon our countenance and traces indelible patterns of refinement upon our character.

"Unfortunately, I am of a critical turn of mind together with a pernicious inclination to believe with the ancient Greeks that an ugly body houses an ugly soul and that loveliness dwells only in beautiful temples.

"Certainly, certainly this inclination has led me into more than one blind alley. Ah, if I could only wield the pen as skillfully as I can this—" He flourished a carving knife, for we were at a table and he was occupied at the moment in carving the *pièce de résistance.* "I would tell the world how untrue my premise is. And what a cruel fallacy outer loveliness ofttimes proves itself to be.

"Despite this, my contrary nature clings like a leech to the belief that beautiful temples are invariably beautiful within.

"And it chanced, I say chanced, since there is the probability that someone not half so lovely might have done the same deed, and had such been the case my belief would have suffered a terrible set-back. It chanced that the loveliest woman I ever saw was the most beautiful.

"I saw her first under amazing circumstances. Circumstances so extraordinary they seem unreal to this day, but I won't linger upon them, because they make another story. My second sight of her was in a crowded court-room and it was then while she sat very primly upon the culprit's bench that I had my first opportunity really to see her.

"She was a little woman. Feel as you like towards all other types, but a little woman has appeal. Especially, a little old woman with silvery hair, and an unnameable air about her, that is like fingers forever playing upon the chords of sweetest memories. All this, and a prettiness beside, a trifle faded of course, but dainty and fragile and lovely—rare, you might say, as a bit of old, old lace. And kindliness overlaying this, to lend a charm to her beauty that jewel or raiment could not render. Her silvery hair crinkled almost to the point of that natural curliness which Negro blood imparts. The kind of curl that no artificial aid so far invented can duplicate. Her eyes were extremely heavy-lidded, which is, as you know, a purely Negro attribute, and her mouth had a fullness, a ripeness, exceedingly—*African.*

"That she was anything other than a white American was improbable, improbable indeed. She, the widow of old Colonel Ritton, deceased, of Westview. As dauntless and intrepid a figure as ever lived to make history for his country. His career as an Indian fighter, pioneer and brave, open opposer of the lawlessness which held sway over the far West in the late sixties is a thing that is pointed to with pride and made much of, by Americans. Three notable sons, high standing in their respective vocations, paid her the homage due the mother of such stalwart, upright men as themselves. Two daughters, fêted continuously because of their beauty, were married into families, whose family-tree flourished like the proverbial mustard-seed, unblighted before the world.

"There had to be some reason why a lady of her standing was forced to appear in court. The truth is, it was not because of the greatness of her offense; but because of the unusualness of her misconduct which had raised such a hue and cry; until drastic methods had to be resorted to.

"The charge against her was one of several counts, the plaintiffs being three very stout gentlemen, florid-faced, heavy-jowled, wide-paunched to a man. Each of them diffused a pomposity; which while being imposing managed somehow to be amusing. Their very manner bespoke their grim determination to punish the defendant. Their portly bodies fairly bristled with the strength of this intention. The muscles in their heavy faces worked as though the currents of their thoughts were supplied by volts of wonderment, shocking and bewildering. They charged, first: That the defendant willfully hampered them in the fulfillment of their authorized duty. Second: That the defendant had knowingly aided a criminal to evade the hands of the law, by sheltering the said criminal in or about her premises. Third: That the defendant had spoken untruthfully with intent to deceive by denying all knowledge of said criminal's whereabouts. Fourth: That the concealment of said criminal constituted a tort; the criminal being of so dangerous a character, his being at liberty was a menace to the commonwealth."

Timothy Phipps paused, as he busied himself, serving generous slices of baked ham to his guests. In the act of laying a copious helping upon his own plate, he commenced again, to unreel his yarn.

"There is no joy in life so satisfying, so joyous, as that of having our belief strengthened—to watch iridescent bubbles—our castles in the air—settle, unbroken upon firm old earth. To hear our doubts go singing through the chimneys of oblivion. Ah, that's joy indeed. And it is what I experienced that never-to-be forgotten day in the dinkiest little court-room in the world.

"A rainy spell was holding sway and a penetrating drizzle oozed from the sky as though the clouds were one big jelly-bag hung to drip, drip, drip. I was sogged with depression; what with the weather and the fact that I was marooned in a very hostile section of my native land, it was little wonder that my nerves were jumpy and a soddenness saturated my spirits, even though I knew that the fugitive was free and, making a rough guess at it, was to remain so. But an emotion more impelling than curiosity forced me to linger to witness the outcome of old Mrs. Ritton's legal skirmish.

"From a maze of judicial meanderings, these facts were made known.

"The old Ritton house was a big rambling structure built at some period so long ago, the time was forgotten. It was not a place of quick escapes, for no such thing as fleeing fugitives had been thought of, in its planning. Unexpected steps up and steps down made hasty flight hazardous. Unlooked-for corners and unaccountable turns called for leisurely progress and long halls with closed doors at their furtherest end, opening into other chambers, were hindrances no stranger could shun. All told, the house as it stood was a potent witness against the defendant; each of its numerous narrow-paned windows screeched the fact that none but the initiated could play at hide-and-seek within its walls.

"Many pros and cons were bandied about as to why the runaway Negro had entered Ritton's house. That he had done an unwonted thing went without saying—since hunted things flee to the outposts of Nature, shunning human habitation as one does a pestilence: to the long, long road girt by a clear horizon, where dipping sky meets lifting earth, on, on to the boundless space, away to the forest where wild things hover, or a dash to the mountains to seek out sheltering cave and cavern.

"At first, it was thought that entering the Ritton house was a 'dodge' but subsequent happenings had proven the supposition false. It was quite clear that he had gone in for protection and had found it.

"The claimants carefully explained to the court, how they had

chased the Negro down Anthony, up Clements and into Marvin, the
street which ran north and south beneath the Ritton-house windows.
They were not but a few lengths behind the fugitive—not close
enough, you understand, to lay hold upon him; nor so near that they
could swear that someone signalled from an open window in the Ritton house. How-be-it, they saw the Negro swerve from the street,
dart through the Rittons' gate, dash down the walk, and enter the
Ritton house. Less than five minutes afterwards they, themselves,
pursued the Negro step by step into the building; to find upon entering it a room so spacious that the several pieces of fine old furniture arranged within it did not dispel an effect of emptiness, while
the brilliant light of early afternoon showered upon everything,
sparklingly, as if to say, 'No place to hide in here' and over beside an
open window old lady Ritton sat very calmly, knitting. And upon
being questioned she had strenuously denied that a black man had
preceded them into her chamber.

"Finally the point was reached, when the defendant took the
stand. And the Lord knows, so much depended, that is, as far as I was
concerned, upon what she would or would not say—well, what she
said makes my story.

"'Gentlemen, the thing you desire me to tell you, I cannot.
Though, I think if I could make you understand a little of my feel-
ings, you will cease—all of you being gentlemen—endeavoring to
force me to divulge my secret.

"'You, all of you, have been born so unfettered that you have responded to your every impulse; perhaps it will be hard to realize the
gamut of my restraint, when I swear to you, gentlemen, that in all
my life, I have experienced no great passion and responded to the
urge of only two impulses—two—but two—and these, gentlemen,
have become for me a sacred trust.

"'It was years ago when I felt the first impulse and answered it.
It has no apparent connection with the present occurrence. Yet, possibly, for no other reason than an old lady's imagining, the mem-

ory of that first occasion has leaped across the years to interlace itself with this.

"'Wait, gentlemen. I will tell you all about it. This turbulence has
awakened old dreams and old longings and opened the doors of
yester-years in the midst of an old lady's musing; but it is worth all
the worry. Yes, 'tis worth it.

"'It is strange what mighty chains are forged by impulses and none
of us know the strength that is required to break them. My first impulse wrought me much of happiness—very much happiness, gentlemen. Bear with an old lady's rambling—your Honor, and I shall
relate just how it happened.

"'I was ten years old, when my master—

"'Pardon? Yes? Yes, sirs—My master.

"'I was ten years old; when my master gave up his small holdings
in the South and came West with his family, his wife—my mistress—
a daughter and two sons and myself. We traveled what was then the
tortuous trail that begins east of the Mississippi and ended in the
rolling plains beside the Rio Grande. Our trip lasted a fortnight
longer than we expected or had planned for. Once along the way, we
were robbed. Again, we were forced to break camp and flee because
a warring band of Indians was drawing near. Afterwards, we found to
our dismay, that a box of provisions had been forgotten or had been
lost. Misfortune kept very close to us throughout our journey, our
food was all but gone. There was wild game for the killing, but am-
munition was too precious to be squandered in such manner. Master
had already given the command that we were to hold in our stom-
achs and draw in our belts until we reached some point where we
could restock our fast dwindling supplies.

"'One day, an hour before sundown, we struck camp in a very
lovely spot—a sloping hillside covered with dwarf cedars and scrub
oaks, a hillside that undulated and sloped until it merged into a sandy
golden-bottomed ravine. We pitched our camp in a sheltered nook in
this ravine. The golden sand still warm from the day's sunshine made

a luxurious resting place for our weary bodies. Below us, a spring trickled up through the earth and spread like lengths of sheerest silk over the bed of sand.

"'In a little while our camp-fire was sending up curling smoke-wreaths, smoke-blue into the balmy air, and a pot of boiling coffee—our very last—added its fragrance to the spice of cedars and the pungency of oaks. Sundown came on, and a great beauty settled over everything. Nature was flaunting that side of herself which she reveals to the wanderer in solitary places: the shy kisses she bestows upon the Mountain's brow and, passion-warmed, glows in flagrant colors of the sunset; the tender embrace with which she wraps the plains and the glistening peace shines again in sparkling stars. Beauty that is serene and beauty that brings peace and calm and happiness and is never found in towns or crowded cities.

"'Our three hounds—faithful brutes that had trailed beside us all the weary miles—sat on their haunches and lifted their heads to send up long and doleful cries into the stillness.

"'"Here—here—" cried Master. "Quit that!—Come, come, we'll take a walk and maybe scare up something to fill the pot tomorrow." He ended by whistling up to the prancing dogs and they were off. Up the hillside they went, the dogs, noses to earth, skulking at Master's heels or plunging into the under-brush on a make-believe scent.

"'I sat in the warm sand, a lonely slave-child, watching Master and the dogs until they reached the hill-top. Almost on the instant, the dogs scared up a rabbit. What a din they made yelping, yip, yap, yap and Master halooing and urging them to the race. The frightened rabbit ran like the wind, a living atom with the speed of a flying arrow. Straight as a shooting star, it sped: until turning suddenly it began bounding back along the way it had come. The ruse worked. The dogs sped past, hot on his trail of the dodging rabbit, many paces forward before they were able to stop short and pick up the scent once more. And the rabbit ran, oh, how he ran tumbling, darting, swirling down the hillside, terror-mad, fright-blind, on he came, the dogs on his trail once more, bounding length over length behind him. One last frantic dash, one desperate leap and the rabbit plunged into my lap. I covered the tiny trembling creature with my hands, just in time, before the great hounds sprang towards me. With great effort I kept them off and managed to conceal my captive in the large old-fashioned pocket of my wide skirt.

"'Master, disgruntled at his dogs and quite ireful—it is no little thing for a hungry man to see a tempting morsel escape him—came up to question me. "That rabbit—that rabbit—which way did it go?"

"'When I replied "Don't know," he became quite angry and beat me. Gentlemen, the scars of that long-ago flogging I shall carry to my grave. Our food was nearly gone and it was I, the slave-girl, who knew the lack most sorely. But I did not give the rabbit over to my master.'

"She paused a little while and in all my life I never before knew such quiet; you could actually feel the silence.

"'It is strange, strange how far reaching the consequences of an impulse may be. Howard, my master's son, witnessed everything. He had always teased me. His favorite pastime had been to annoy the slave-girl with his pranks, but he changed from that day. That day, when he saw his father beat me. And it was he, gentlemen, who taught me to forget the scars of serfdom and taught me the joys of freedom. In all truth, sirs, I am the widow of Colonel Howard Monroe Ritton of Westview.'

"There is no use trying to tell you about that," declared Timothy. "It's an experience as indescribable as it is unforgettable. That little old white-haired woman standing alone in the midst of all those hostile people, tearing apart with such simple words the whole fabric of her life. I think it was her loveliness that held them spell-bound; the power of her beauty, that kept them straining their ears to catch every word she said. As if suddenly awakened to her surroundings, she cleared her throat nervously, and hurriedly concluded her story.

"'The necessity of my being here, gentlemen, is the outcome of my second impulse, an impulse, gentlemen, nothing more. Each afternoon I sit in my west chamber beside my sunny windows, there is a whole beautiful row of them, as one can see by passing along the street . . . I like the sunshine which pours through them of an afternoon, and I like to knit. And I like to watch the passersby. And, I think, gentlemen, whenever I sit there I can recall more easily the things that are passed, the old friends, the old places, the old loves and the old hurts which, somehow, have no longer the power to bring pain.

"'So I was peering—my eyes are not so good—into the street and I saw a cloud of dust, all of a sudden. I thrust my head a little ways through the window, then, I saw a man running; on looking closer, I saw that he was black.

"'Then a queer thing happened, gentlemen; the first time in years on years, I remembered the days of my bondage. And curiously, yes, curiously I recalled. Wait. No, I did not recall it. I swear to you, gentlemen, a picture formed before me; a hilly slope overgrown with trees of scrub oak and dwarf cedars—a golden sand-bottomed ravine and twilight falling upon miles on miles of wind-swept prairie, and peace, sweet and warm and kind, brushing my soul and turning my thoughts towards God. And I heard it, the strident yelps of three strong dogs. I saw it—a tiny furry rabbit running for its life. I tell you—it was real, gentlemen. And while I looked, it faded—changed—glowed into another picture—the one that was being enacted out in the street. It glimmered back to fancy and flashed again to fact, so swiftly, I could not distinguish which. Then, sirs, they merged and both were one. . . . The black man who was running so wildly was only a little terror-mad rabbit. The three stout gentlemen there,' (she pointed, quite like a child toward the fat policemen, while a ripple of laughter floated across the room), 'and the crowd which followed after, very strangely, gentlemen, every person in it had the visage of my master. I think I cried out at that, sirs. Yes. Certainly I cried—at that.

"'Then the black man was in my presence, inside my sunny west chamber, and I was forced to act—act quickly—

"'The picture had to be finished, gentlemen. The rabbit, no, the man—had to be protected. Thank you, sirs. That is all.'

"Yes," said Timothy Phipps, pensively. "I was the running black gentleman in the story—" He tilted his head a bit backwards and sideways and laughed. His laughter echoing—joy—joy—joy!

Crisis 31 (January 1926): 118–122.

The Brat

A WILD NIGHT, a blazing hearth, a rose-lit room, low, sweet music, an over-stuffed armchair and a companion; who can tell a tale of life, as she is: ah, there's charm and warmth and cheer, a-plenty.

The night was not only wild, it was raving, stark, tearing mad. Rain and wind strove together in a fierce onslaught. The wind shrieking and howling like runaway fury. The rain pounding like fifty drummers, each bent on out-drumming his mate.

My room, rose-lit and cheery, the coziest spot I know. My favorite record, playing over and over, tenderly, hauntingly. A chair, over-stuffed and comfortable, stretched out its arms, like a mother's wide flung, to embrace me. But—I was companionless. Yet—It is not given unto you or to me to have all things at all times.

A KNOCK. A clattering banging, biff-booming, biff-booming. It had to be, to become distinguishable from the drum-beats of the rain.

What? Who—who? Without on a night like this?

Come in—Come in—Come in.

And in limped old Jennie.

Old Jennie, all twisted and bent with premature age, which wrapped her about like an ill-fitting garment; which wrinkled her skin and whitened her hair, but did not reflect itself in her eyes. Old Jennie's eyes were marvelous. They sparkled in her wrinkled face like gems—the gems of youth. Nor did her age lessen her activity. Bent and lame as she was, she worked amazingly, accomplishing the labors of three women with speed that was unbelievable. She was a silent creature, speaking only when speech was imperative and then in the fewest words. Her voice had a haunting quality, a resonance, a something that vaguely stirred some chord, a memory, though indefinable; like a whiff of fragrance from a forgotten perfume. I have never seen old Jennie smile. Yet, in her presence there is no trace of gloom, no hint of sadness. And her eyes so sparkling, so youthful, have often caused me to idly wonder.

She came upon me now, as surprisingly as a genie from Aladdin's lamp. Old silent Jennie out of the night and the storm into my rose-lit room, dripping wet, and to my utter surprise, quite full of words.

"It's only me, Miss Aggie, only me. 'Twas my day up to the Towers and the storm—Ain't it the worse you ever saw? Overtook me on my way home, right herein this neighborhood, where I felt like a rat a-gettin' drowned, 'til I remembered you and 'lowed how you would give me shelter 'til the storm pass."

A night for surprises, indeed. Old Jennie esteeming me above my fellows. A pleasing surprise bobbing up to nod at me like daisies on a hillside. A pleasing, warming, cheering surprise that old Jennie, old black Jennie, old wash-woman, scrub-woman, ugly, wrinkled, old, old thing esteemed me above my fellows. Straightway my thoughts turned to a warm robe, padded silken mules and woolen hose, and they were surprises for Jennie. Oh, what a night for surprises!

Presently Jennie and I were sitting before my hearth. And such a blaze was roaring up the chimney.

"How jolly to have you with me, Jennie. How glad I am you thought of me," said I.

"Humph!" rejoined old Jennie.

We sat there, my old wash-woman and I, a long, long while saying nothing. Then suddenly Jennie spoke:

"Miss Aggie, that music, that music is making me want to tell you somethin' I ain't never told nobody before. Somethin' no other living person knows but me. And its true, true, true: God knows it's true."

She paused and I did not break the silence. I fancied it was not me she was talking to. She was answering the magic of my rose-lit room, the glowing warmth, the music, yes, most of all the music. So I remained quiet in my best of chairs and waited.

"I ain't no old, old woman like I seems. The number of my years ain't many. Not many, Miss Aggie. If you just count time. But if you reckons the days I've spent in sorrow and pain and regrets then I'm old, old, old.

"I was young and wild. So wild and young when the riot occurred. It ain't no call for tellin' dates or naming places, it's just one bitter fact I'm mindful of. As for the riot there hasn't ever been one so bad since and it weren't never one so bad before. Black folk were butchered and slaughtered right and left and white folks—Well, the black folks fought back that's what made it a riot. I was young, but I wasn't too young to be a mother. A wild young thing and a mother.

"My baby. I can see him now, as he was then. Little trusting mite. My baby. He was one year old. 'Twas his birthday, that day of the riot. Baby, my baby, is what I call him now, but then I called him 'the brat'—just that. I had no other name to give him. No love for him was in my heart, and his father wouldn't dast to own him.

"It all comes from my being born what I am and from those a-fore me, and I guess those a-fore them. My ma had so many children her one concern was to name us and parcel us out. We were scattered like a litter of kittens, here, there and everywhere. But it never came my turn to go. Maybe it was because I could sing, and singing I earned money to help keep body and soul together.

"You don't know the bitterness of being born poor. It ain't the things you ain't got and the havin' to do without and the needin' and the wantin' that crushes the heart out of you. It's the meanness, the littleness and the pettiness which poverty breeds. It's the tiny splinter lost in the flesh that festers quickest, and being poor is that-a-way—it festers.

"I could sing. So I was sent out into the street to pick up nickels and dimes a-singin'. Pretty soon I'd learned other ways to wheedle coins from those who were untouched by my voice.

"My voice was God-given. I got proof of that. Even if I did use it to carry me to the devil. To the devil I went faster than a pine knot burns. Gettin' wilder and wilder. Payin' no sort 'er attention to anybody. Proud of my singing, proud of my looks, proud of my wildness. Until the time come when I didn't have a friend, when I wasn't even fit to sing 'fore folks, when I didn't have a crust of bread to eat nor shoes to stick my feet into. Then a girl called Biddy befriended me and stood by me through all my trouble.

"I had seen her often, when I was too proud to notice her kind. A fair, fair girl she was, with big blue eyes and straw-colored hair. Nobody noticed her looks. 'Cause it is common, a common sight enough to see colored folks as white as white folks, and women to see it the other way 'round, too. 'The brat' was a-goin' to be one or the other of that kind.

"Biddy was a queer one with a reputation for using genteel language and of never being known to cheat. She had a kind of humble O-I-want-to-please-you air about her that made her the laughing-stock of folks in our district. She drank like a fish and I suspect she used something else. It's true, she was a queer one, and to top it all she lived with Black Luke, a big burly man as mean as sin and as black as night. When he was a-mind to, he beat her awful. Then, for weeks and weeks afterwards, he'd be kind to her, showing his teeth like a snarling dog at anyone who dared to so much as speak to her. They loved each other all right, and they stuck together through thick and thin. And they shared their home with me. 'The brat' was born under their roof.

"Biddy loved him from the first. And she nursed him and tended him and kept him clean. She coaxed Black Luke to buy him little trinkets and pretty little dresses and socks and shoes. She called him 'Little brat' like I did, but when she said it, soft and sweet-like, it sounded like a caress—'Little brat—Little brat.'

"We lived together all of that awful year and Biddy used to tell us about her folks, always with a sort 'er reverence that made you pity her. She told me their names and where they lived so many, many times, I learned 'em like I did my a, b, c's. Then the day came, when 'the brat' was one year old, that day of the riot, and we grown-ones celebrated the occasion with drink. I was dead drunk, too drunk to know or to care how or why they were a-fightin' out in the street.

"Black Luke had one of his mean fits and he was sure one man to fear whenever he had one. It seems most like a bad dream but I'm mighty certain he beat Biddy before he drank himself to sleep sitting upright on the floor with his head leant back 'gainst the wall.

"Yes, that part of it is dim like things seen at twilight, before it goes all dark. What I remember is the thick black pressing gloom that fell on me that day. I don't know yet how the riot started; but I know that it was awful. Smoke and fire. Smoke and fire and screams and shouts and pitiful cries for help help help. A-hearing God's name blasphemed one minute and the next minute a-listening to His name going up in prayer. Rocks, sticks, bricks and pistol-shots flyin' through the air and people, men, women, and little children, a-scamperin' back and forth like frightened mice, and others, men, women, and little children, gone mad with tasting blood, fighting like savage beasts and all the while Biddy and Black Luke and 'the brat' and me huddled like stupid sheep in our room. There was Biddy sitting stiffly in a chair with my 'flesh and blood' in her arms, staring straight ahead, straight before her, just staring. And

Black Luke asleep on the floor, with his head a-restin' 'gainst the wall.

"Bang, whiz, thud. A bullet spat over me and found its mark in Black Luke's head. He groaned once, toppled over and was still. Another bullet followed and another and another. Someone stood outside a-firin' until their pistol was empty.

"Biddy said: 'Oh, God—God—God!' Six times just that-a-way. Then she was still too, so still, so still. 'The brat' roused in her arms and whimpered. A tongue of flame licked through our roof. It was awful.

"When the fire had burned half way cross, Biddy got up so calm and yet eager, like a young girl goin' out on a ball-room floor to dance. She wrapped an old shawl 'bout my baby and put on her hat. Then she went to Black Luke's body and knelt beside it. She kissed him a long, long kiss on his cooling lips, and her hand over him, slow-like, tender-like, gentle-like. Then she quit that and went to searching in his pockets, first one and then the other, until she has thrust her hand into every one. But each time they come out empty. She tore open the front of his shirt, a-feelin' all in there. And still her hands were empty. She began to move her lips, a-praying. And tears streamed down her cheeks. She reached for his hat that had fallen off his head, when he toppled, and began a-feelin' inside it. She pulled out the band, her hands all trembly and a-fumblin' in her eagerness. Presently she drew out money, paper money, I don't know how much; then she began to laugh. A funny, funny laugh with tears streaming down her cheeks. She put the money into her bosom, down in between her corset, and came over to me and said, still laughing a little in that funny, funny way, with tears streaming down her cheeks:

"'Jen, you're such a sot, it does not matter if you are killed—I wish I could be, too. But "the brat," somebody's got to save "the brat." I'm going to take him home. Home. Where he'll be cared for and allowed to grow clean like he ought. He is little. Too little to remember all the dirt he's seen. And with my folks he'll have a chance to be a man. Do you hear, Jennie, girl—a man? That's why I'm going to wade through blood—going through that hell out there, to carry him home. Jennie, listen to me—listen, girl—that's why I'm leaving you—to carry him home—to my own folks—home—'

"She stooped then and give me a quick kiss. I recollects how I rubbed it away, a-thinkin' 'bout that long, long one she'd just given Black Luke, and him dead.

"Young I was and wild and foolish and a sot; so I lay there befuddled with drink while she carried my baby away. For an instant I was glad, glad to be shed of 'the brat' forever. He had cost me dear. Something had gone wrong with my voice since his coming. And nobody, except Biddy, had been kind to me. Only Biddy.

"Then suddenly I realized that Biddy was gone—gone. I seemed to know for the first time what that tongue of flame a-lickin' across the roof over my head meant and that poor Black Luke was a-lyin' dead, almost at my feet; and I heard the screaming outside, and the firing. But all I could think of was, Biddy had gone—Biddy, who was kind to me—Biddy had gone and left me trapped in a burning house, with a dead man. I screamed and screamed. Come back, come back, Biddy, come back! And screaming I ran to the window that had been shattered with bullets.

"I got there in time to see a man aim his gun at Biddy. Saw him pull the trigger. Heard the shot. And as sure as God's in heaven, it struck Biddy; but Biddy kept on a-goin'. I screamed. It seemed that never, so long as I lived, would I ever quit screaming—screaming—screaming.

"They picked me up from where I had fallen through the window. The fall made me a cripple but it didn't kill me. Why—why—why? When I didn't have a single thing to live for? Why, when other women, pure and good—true wives and loving mothers—were slaughtered that day like pigs in a pen? But it was six months before I could leave the hospital, and when I did my voice was gone completely. Six months before I could even start to get ready to go after 'the brat'—my baby.

"I hadn't ever cared for him or wanted him before. Now my heart ached for him, day and night. I think it was the cool, quiet, cleanness all about me, the easy-steppin' doctors and the pretty lady nurses, and the peacefulness, after that awful, awful day, that changed me. I spent all the long hours a gettin' well, a-picturin' the way he crinkled his face to smile. How it took all his baby fingers to wrap 'round one of mine. Recallin' one by one his cunnin' baby tricks. And wantin' him so hard, it hurt, like pain.

"Well, I set about earning my fare to Biddy's home. And I was bent on being presentable, too. I didn't want Biddy's folks a-shame of me. She had talked so much about 'em, I felt I knew the kind 'er folks they'd be. A-lyin' there in the hospital with so much time to think and a-lookin' back. I saw things I hadn't noticed before and some that I had noticed but never heeded, and it made me feel like my folks would'er been their kind if—Well, you know, I felt that-a-way, a-lyin' there. Plain, honest, decent, and mighty proud-like, 'cause God had let you be so. Such thoughts and one thing and another and the gettin' money to go and a whole year had slipped by.

"It was night when I got there, but I went straight to Biddy's home—straight to Biddy's folks. And oh, my God! Miss Aggie, they were white—white folks. White, Miss Aggie, like you. But I wanted my baby. So I mentioned Biddy's name. It was like a pass-word. They welcomed me and treated me ever and ever so nice. I saw my baby and played with him and kissed him—God knows I didn't keep count of the times I kissed him in the little while I had the chance.

"Biddy was dead—shot. Just like I knew. She had lived long enough to put my baby in her mother's arms. And her not knowing, supposed 'the brat' belonged to Biddy. They were glad to have him—'the Brat,' my baby—because they thought he was a little mite of living flesh, sprung from their own—their daughter, to whom they had been harsh, too strict, too hard. They gloried in the chance they'd been given to make it all up to her through her child.

"And when I saw how clean my baby was, and how healthy he was and wholesome, and all the things they were doin' for him that I could never do, I pretended I was his old nurse, come to see him, 'cause I had loved his mother before him and couldn't help feelin' interested-like in her child. Oh, I set there, a-tellin' 'em lies and lies and lies, while my heart was breakin', and when I could bear it no more I ups and left—and left 'the brat,' too.

"It's funny how easy a heart can break, as easy as an egg-shell, only an egg-shell breaks but once and a heart mends—mends to break again. So it was from the first; in another year, after I left 'the brat,' I went back to see him again—'lowing I was his old nurse droppin' in for the sake of his mother.

"I made a lot of that lovin' his mother, 'cause I did love Biddy—I love her yet. She was kind to me when nobody else was. And seeing my baby thrive and grow sweeter every year made me grateful. And I remembered her words: 'Jen, you're such a sot, it does not matter if you are killed.' So I started goin' straight and keepin' straight 'cause of her wantin' so much to have 'the brat' grow clean and wholesome.

"I kept it up, a-goin' back every year. Workin' hard and savin' my money, so's to buy my boy gifts. A-breakin' my heart over and over until my boy was twelve years old.

"For a long time his playmates had been a-teasin' him 'bout his 'ol' black mammy.' Poking fun at him and a-laughin'. He stood it, though, 'til he was twelve years old. That's when my heart broke its last time. It can never break any more. It's still and dead, 'cause it didn't break to mend, the time my boy refused to see me. Even when Biddy's folks forced him to come shake hands, he wouldn't look at me, wouldn't let me kiss him. And wouldn't take my gifts—not one.

"Like a slap in the face I minded the moment when I'd been mighty glad to be shed of 'the brat' forever. My baby—my baby. I grit my teeth, and I tried to pray, and I ain't never been back no more.

"I work, so's I won't have time to think; but I can't get rid of knowing about my boy. It's queer how fore-knowing a mother's heart can be. And this heart of mine that ain't had nothing 'cept breaks and breaks, knows my boy is happy and knows when my boy is sad. He ain't happy now and I'm powerless. He ain't happy and it's me who is to blame—me—who never bothered to mother him when I had the chance; who lay stupid drunk while another woman gave up her life to save him from death or a life far worse.

"I told you 'bout my singin'. Well, my boy sings, too. It's his singin' that's a-turnin' to be his curse. His voice that tells you what he is, is the thing that keeps him bound. He sings like only one of my race can sing, but he sings so fine, so fine, Biddy's race won't let him go.

"His skin is dark and his hair is curly, and his eyes are like mine was in the days when I was young and wild. But they don't betray him none. He's bound—he's bound. Oh, my tears are washed out of my eyes crying for him, but I can't loose his chains.

"It's his singing. He's known in every nook and corner. Children know his name and quit their play to listen to his singin'. Everywhere I go somebody's a-hummin' or whistlin' the songs he sings. Somebody's playin' one of his records—like that one now. Like that one now."

Electrified, I started up, repeating her words like a parrot. Old Jennie sat gazing into the fire. The tense lines of her face, the rigidness of her body, made me think of a marble statue of Truth. A statue come to life, to experience the burning pain of all humanity's pretense and subterfuge and lies.

If she heard my query she gave no heed. So I settled back, in my best of chairs, wonderingly, staring wide-eyed at old Jennie. Staring. Wondering. Tensely aware of music, playing tenderly, hauntingly, "I Hear You Calling Me." My favorite song, sung by my best loved tenor. David Kane, one of America's greatest singers. So young and gifted, of whom America is so arrogantly proud. Proud, that he is no foreigner, come to us from across the sea, but truly ours. A product of America.

Yes, he is dark; but his boyhood home is on the western plains, where unfettered winds blew free, to tan his cheek. True, his dark, coarse hair grows in curly ringlets, but curly hair is ofttimes the only outward mark of genius.

> *I hear you calling me,*
> *And oh, the ringing gladness of your voice.*

Again, old Jennie spoke harshly, bitterly, her voice laden with poignant sorrow that poured over me a torrent of heart-rending grief.

"Listen, listen, any fool knows that ain't no white man's voice. He's mine, he's mine, he's mine. As true as God's in heaven, he's mine, Miss Aggie, he's mine."

The drumming rain and the shrieking wind seemed very far, like some hidden chorus in a play of torture. The music trilled through the rose-lit room:

> *You called me when the moon had veiled her light,*
> *Before I went from you into the night.*

Once more old Jennie spoke. And her voice was the croon of a mother. "He's like a little bird caged with lions. He's lonely, so lonely. His poor heart aches and he can't tell why."

> *And my heart*
> *Still hears the distant music of your voice—*
> *I hear you calling me.*

Suddenly, with one move of her crippled body, old Jennie leaped from her chair, flinging her arms wide in a hopeless gesture. Whispering words so pain-seared they scorched:

"Miss Aggie, he hears the call of a race. I tell you his race, and his poor old mother callin', a-callin' him."

***

A LOG CRACKED and settled upon the embers, showering sparks almost at our feet. In the brighten glow, while my eyes were full upon her, for a second's fleeting flight, old Jennie's face was the face of David Kane, America's world-famed tenor.

Messenger 8 (April 1926): 105–106, 126.

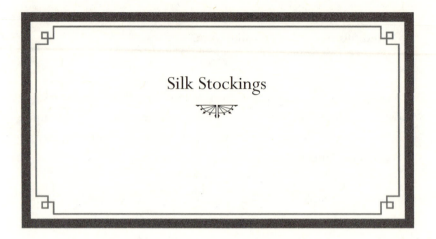

Silk Stockings

THIS IS A PLAIN TALE of plain people. Have you ever thought about it. . . . How the grand, somebody folks are responsible for all the scandal to be found in yellow journals and the poor nobody folks supply the sob-sisters with material for their columns. . . . But for tragedies from which drama is woven, go to plain everyday folks. . . . For humor, the essence of comedy, ditto—go to plain folks. . . . The reason why, here in a nutshell, is; because plain folks never stage their acts. . . . They do not know, so plain are they, that all of tragedy and all of comedy is in each hour of their daily lives. . . .

"There are chords in the human heart, strange varying strings which are only struck by accident." (Accident, no time to stage the effect.) "Which will remain mute and senseless to appeals the most passionate and earnest and respond at last to the slightest casual touch"—(casual, just common, you know.) "In the most insensible or childish minds there is some train of reflection, which art can seldom lead or skill assist; but which will reveal itself, as great truths have done, by chance." There . . . you have the gist of this story. . . . Unless you wish, you need not read on. . . .

Silk stockings are plain things—that is, to some. . . . And to others, silk stockings belong in the class with grand somebody folks. . . . And to others; silk stockings are sob-sister material. . . .

To a very young person named Nancy Meade, silk stockings were so plain things they were dove-tailed into her mind as necessities along with bread and meat.

To young strapping John Light silk stockings were—well, his mother never wore them. . . .

To the plain villain in this plain tale silk stockings at so much per, were handy articles for appropriating admiration for oneself or for fanning the flames of adoration, as you like, in another. . . .

Little Nancy earned her living by dancing as it was her only paying asset, it's plain enough to anybody, why. . . . But she had the reputation of being a good little thing. And all the other girls in "Oh, You Chocolate Dolls," the cheap troupe with which she was booked, called her "The kid" and barring the sheerist mite of raillery which being feminine, at times had a "cattish" trend, let her alone. . . . All the men respected her. . . . Proving that they did so by their immovable reluctance about footing any little bill she might have incurred at an after-the-show-supper or for an off-stage, in between acts—sandwich.

And Nancy not having the means to foot many extras herself kept dutifully at home—"Home" being any place at which the troupe put up—and in quite lady-like manner plying her needle. Nancy's dissipation was clothes. Pretty clothes . . . ravishing clothes . . . silken clothes. She adored fine laces and thick plushy velvets and she possessed a ferret's nose for scenting out the most expensive and the most exquisite garments in any man's shop. . . . So, the clothes she wore were the sort homely women dream about. . . . Clothes that made her co-workers green with envy. . . . She didn't have money, but she had the knack of putting clothes together with a needle and thread—Her clothes made the chambermaids at the varying hotels pop their eyes and clothes that made women she passed on the street turn about for a second, sometimes even a third, stare. . . .

Nancy was certainly nimble-fingered to a marked degree as well as quick on her toes. . . . She did a great deal of mending, ripping, letting out, altering and remaking. At times she even dyed and pressed lingerie, blouses and dresses; but silk stockings are peculiar things. . . .

Nancy just couldn't make silk stockings. . . . Nor could she alter them—rip them up and make them over. . . . Of course, she might have darned them; but who, being a lover of silk hose, wishes to darn them? Who versed in the oddities of silk stockings, even wants to darn them? Whatever your arguments, Nancy did not.

She bought silk stockings like a thoroughbred, wore them like a queen, and discarded them, when they threatened a "run," like any other devotee.

Nancy earned all she got. I have told you how. But she did not get much and with a penchant for finery and an especial longing for silken hosiery. . . . Raise the curtain please . . . here comes the villain.

Gerald Lincoln McKay; do not be glad to meet. . . .

Gerald had kept no accurate account of his "scalps," the term he used for his numerous lady-loves with whom he had played around and discarded. He was actually a connoisseur of ladies . . . and just as cold-blooded in his tactics with them as any critical judge of antiques and art. He spoke of the gentler sex as types. . . . He would say:

"That Mrs. West. . . . Ah, yes. . . . Your red-hot mamma type. . . . Little Elfie Sanders . . . sure I know her . . . real baby type. . . . Ida Moss. . . . By the way, there now, is your Kitten type. . . . He would stroke his long chin and run his eyes over a roomful of girls and comment: "Not an innocent type here—la, la, that kind's passing."

Few men enjoyed his presence. But the devil having engineered his transportation into this realm had seen to it, that he pleased the ladies. His was a long sallow face, ivory-colored. . . . His was the hair women delight to pass their hands through, soft, and thick, and wavy, and he kept it scented. . . . And he possessed that indeterminate orb, which poets call soulful. . . .

Speaking of his eyes. . . . "There'd come a moment," the girls said . . . ."When you would be studying 'bout. . . . Oh, nothing at all and you'd glance up at Gerald"—he was gracefully tall.—"And you'd feel—oh, you couldn't explain it—and the next thing you'd be—according to your type—hugging him or he'd be hugging you. . . ."

As you might know the innocent type was Gerald's particular prey. . . . It did him good. Gave a zest to his life. . . . Kept him keen for battle. . . . Sharpened his weapons. . . . Appeased his appetite to prove the innocent little things not innocent at all. . . .

At first sight of Nancy, Gerald girthed himself for battle.

He really had a way with women. . . . And Nancy was soon glowing and beaming under his expert tutelage.

That love transforms a woman is not altogether true; because a woman can love most earnestly a thousand years; if that were possible, and none would ever know it, so far as any difference it may make in her ability to scintillate and dazzle; but give her a lover, one who feeds her vanity; now then, we have the secret of the transformation.

Nancy was not in love with Gerald, thank heaven. Yet, probably time would have wrought real havoc had not Providence moved John Silas Light straight onto the stage . . . when the scene was set for the entrance of the hero.

John Silas Light, a torch-bearer. Perhaps you have never heard of him and have never caught the glimmer of his torch. Often, girls had declared to one another: "They wouldn't have him. He is too slow" . . . but each had locked in the closed chamber of her heart, the fervent hope; that beneath her fiancée's dashing qualities, were hidden and waiting for marriage to reveal them, the sterling attributes of a John Silas Light.

He is likely to be the fellow who goes to work at six o'clock every morning and eats lunch from a tin-pail at noon, finding the cold lumpy food palatable; because "his old gal" prepared it. He goes straight home, when he is off the job, and once there, he is apt to become ridiculous while at play with a couple of kids. . . . For strangely enough, considering his length and girth, he can conform his proportions to a ginger-bread-man's or a squealing pig's and he can march and growl like Bruin, the bear. And, too, he is a bit of a bore always annoying the gang with harping about his wife and his wonder-baby; but then, you can borrow a portion of his pay-check and so long as he thinks you "square," he will go hungry before ever asking you to "hand" it back. And without really meaning to, you fall into the habit of letting your troublesome ten-year-old spend his evenings over to his house. . . . Rests you so, to have him some safe place out of the way. . . . Besides, all the other young-sters in the neighborhood are there.

Nancy's John Silas Light revered all women—smile if you want to—because his mother was; as was the Holy Virgin, a woman. He hated to see women carrying bundles or cranking cars, he always wanted to assist them; and, because often, he could not, owing to convention and because of color, made all there was of pathos in his plain existence.

As often as not, he over-stepped convention in a straight-forward, big-hearted way. But he could neither side-step nor over-step color, and to attempt "stepping on it" was like stepping upon a puncture-proof air mattress; it merely bulged in another place. So, he was rapidly becoming soured. The warping things of life often does that to the John Silas Lights; just as time and heat turns sweet milk to clabber.

He was becoming worn as an old shoe is worn and he needed polishing and brightening up. . . . And what better than to have a blithe, pretty creature like Nancy dance right into his heart?

John sat in the front row and watched Nancy's face or perhaps, all of her winsome body, instead of just her legs. . . . He thought her adorable.

And Nancy, strange as it may sound, saw John from across the

foot-lights and straightway forgot to perform for her audience. . . .
She began dancing just for him. . . .

Yes. . . . It was done . . . the portrayal of your hero and heroine's
love-making; but it takes too fine writing for this plain tale. . . .

Hence:——John and Nancy were married the forthcoming Spring
as soon as her contract ended.

And, mind you, John didn't even have the ciphers to a bank account, nor did he give a single fig for silk stockings. . . .

John was a worshipper of women and as most worshippers are,
had not the wit to discover why they were so easy to worship. It's a
common saying, that when a woman is ugly it is her own fault. A
louse can interpret the meaning; but not so John. . . . Such a cue as
the following gave no light to him. . . . There's a cream for every
face. . . . A style for every figure. . . . Fabrics to match the style and
colors to match complexions. . . . And where is the leg that is un-
sightly in a nice silk stocking?

A moral daubed on at the end spoils any good story; but taking it
right in the middle hits the nail on the head and it drives in without
hurting a thumb. The moral is here, but find it. . . .

John was inordinately happy. He forgot to sulk because the Cre-
ator had run into dark colors when he happened along. . . . In due
time, he threw all doubts, all fears, and all precautions to the four
winds and became a father.

Blithe Nancy emerged from the ordeal in no wit daunted. She
was as girlishly rounded as ever; as nimble upon her toes as ever and
far more eager for pretty new clothes. . . .

Many of her prenuptial garments had been cut up and done over
into the prettiest, cunningest baby things you ever saw. . . . You can't
blame Nancy for expecting a whole new outfit for herself as soon as
this baby-business was over. She did not get it. . . . She cast subtle
hints and talked largely of all her clothes being "rags" and complain-
ing childishly "that she didn't have a thing to wear. . . ." All to no use.

Then, in a desperate moment, she quite matter of factly, asked
John to buy her some stockings. . . .

Now, John's mother was a thick stoutish, old-fashioned lady who did not believe silk was silk unless it "rustled," and had all her life encased her legs in cotton. John, manifesting the contrariness of man, immediately, upon hearing Nancy's request, settled his thoughts upon the stockings his mother had worn and never once thought of—he could have looked for that matter—the stockings his wife was wearing.

That evening he gave Nancy the stockings which he had dutifully bought. . . . Hanging about wistfully to watch her unwrap them, so that he might witness her delight. . . . But Nancy was yet coy enough not to. She waited to be alone and one glance at them . . . those awful stockings! made her cry herself to sleep.

Next morning, for the first time since her marriage, Nancy began an appraisal of "This man I now wed." A fatal moment in the lives of married folks. A ripe moment for Love to set his thumb to his nose, spread his wings and fly out of the window to escape Satan, who enters the door. . . .

Completely out of sorts and bitter because of the scurvy trick life had played her. . . . Scurvy? It was worse, if she was never to have any more nice things to wear. Why—what was the use in living?

She put Baby to sleep and ran out to the grocery. One had to go on eating and drinking. . . . Drinking and eating even if they had to wear horrid, horrible stockings. . . . Tears blinded her. She could not see . . . the human fashion-plate that stopped short at sight of her.

"By the Lord, it's Nancy," he exclaimed and set himself to the task—no, art—of making her see him. . . .

Angrily, Nancy dashed the tears from her eyes and quickened her pace. . . . She wouldn't be a weeping pillow . . . not for . . . not for twenty Johns. . . . If he wanted her to be old and ugly. . . . If—

"Why, Gerald! . . ."

"'Lo Nan—Pardon . . . er, ah, er, Mrs.—er, Light."

The name accompanied with a real girlish giggle, supplemented by Nancy.

They entered the Grocer's and Gerald stood by, while she made her purchases. Gerald carried her tiny parcels and walked with her to her gate.

Oh, no, he couldn't possibly "come in." That, he reasoned, was too free and above board. . . . And being free and above board is never good diplomacy when you are weighed down with motives that are about fifty leagues under board.

Gerald felt that John had spoiled his fishing, pushed him away from a mighty lovely stream. . . . And if he could sneak back and muddy the stream, he would be willing to call it "quits." As for Nancy, pshaw, her type was usually flighty. He would be careful not to go too far. All he wanted was to make the "old joker" jealous. It would be wise not to start visiting. The old fool would consider the visits to him. He would never suspect a man who came to his home openly.

Gerald laughed in his sleeve at his own imagining of John asking him to "Come in." Welcoming him in his hearty way. . . . Calling to Nancy to fix a bit to eat. . . . Offering him a cigar. . . . Showing him the baby, bragging, like the donkey that he was. He pictured John following him to the door, down the walk, out to the gate and sending his big voice after him far down the street, calling "Come again. . . ."

Gerald was a clever craftsman, he maneuvered adroitly.

Nancy started slipping out to meet him. They would drop into a "movie" while it was dark and steal out again through the throbbing, people-jammed blackness. They would wander about and find a snug seat in the park where the night-scent from flowers and shrubbery pressed upon them while they exchanged confidences. . . .

"Well, you see if you had stuck to me. . . ."

"Oh, Gerald. . . ."

"You couldn't expect a dub—"

"Now don't you dare say a word 'bout John. . . ."

"I wasn't saying nothin' at all 'bout him" (damning John under his breath). "I was going to say you couldn't expect a dub like me to win anybody like you—"

"Oh, Gerald," mournfully.

"Ah, yes, it's oh, Gerald, but you keep on sticking to that big st—, er John. . . . Why don't you leave him? Come and go with me. . . . Come on, honey. . . . You're not happy. . . . You couldn't be. . . . Answer me, honey. . . ."

There would be a faint sob. . . . Yes, indeed, poor Nancy was unhappy, terribly torn with conflicting emotions. . . . What with actually praying for John to rise up some evening and order her to stay home and see that she obeyed him, instead of saying:—"Don't stay out any later than ten, Nannie. . . . At half past ten to the dot, old Sonny-boy wakes up and yells for you. . . . Enjoy yourself but don't forget the time. . . ." And what with being elated at having Gerald make love to her. . . . Why, it actually proved that she didn't look badly, in cheap horrid clothes, after all.

Anyway, John was doing all he could for her and baby and it didn't really matter even if she was "naked. . . ." Only Gerald did have such exquisite taste. . . . And John—she fancied she could see him sitting at home, alone, his shoes kicked off and his feet in those thick, ridged, speckled socks he wore. . . . Suddenly she wanted to be there also; but under the circumstances, of course, she couldn't be, so instead, she snuggled ever so slightly towards Gerald.

Ever and ever so slightly; but then Gerald was there, strung like a ukelele, waiting for that very, mouse-like movement. With no further ado, he took her in his arms and held her. Merely laughing at her stifled little "don'ts," and expertly wiping away her tears with kisses.

Afterwards: . . . Nancy slipping, darting, even dodging back home. Letting herself cautiously into her own house. Resorting to slyness to cover up her entrance. Shivering like a too-daring mouse whilst making ready to get into bed. The thrills of the evening all drowned in a deluge of panic, lest John awaken. . . . Guilty tears dropping silently against the pillow and finally sleep, dreamless and unbroken, until daylight. . . . Awakening in a drowsy contentment, aware that her head is pillowed upon John's curving arm and that he is snoring outrageously. Leaping up, with the knowledge; that drenched her in a pleasurable shower, that she must make ready his breakfast. . . . Altogether pleased with her plain, humdrum duties—happy to be John's wife. . . .

But later in the day thoughts of the night before smudge her pleasure. . . . She insists to herself that she has acted quite all right. Of course, Gerald knew, she didn't mean a thing. Bolstering her wilted convictions with one of Gerald's glib speeches:

"She needn't be a dead one, just 'cause she was married."

It was later than usual. Each time it got later than usual. Long since, John had "turned in" to lie down beside Sonny-boy so that Sonny would hush crying for her and had dropped off himself, into a heavy slumber. The door was unlocked and only the hall-light left burning. Nancy thought of all this and felt sure she hated John. What right had he to give her so much rope. It was his duty to take care of her just as it was hers to care for Sonny-boy. And what care would she be giving Sonny-boy if she never questioned his coming or his going and accepted everything he did, as a matter of course. "It was John's business to guard his own castle." Gerald's eloquence. . . . She actually believed he would not care—didn't care enough about her to even care what she did. Besides, here she was away from home and it was ever so late and he was at home in bed—of course, he didn't care. . . . Of a sudden, she was replying to Gerald's query, and her answer was—yes.

They had a long way to go. Nancy would not take a cab and Gerald assuming precautions he did not feel, led her a roundabout route, turning numerous corners, crossing many streets, traversing block after block. . . . To while away the time, Gerald said sweet things to Nancy and kept squeezing her hand which lay on his arm.

The moon shone brightly, not giving light, as does the sun—for men to behold minutely but only to dazzle man's vision with a radiance.

Even the houses Nancy passed were washed in radiance and sketched into the tapestry of night, beautiful as fairy-places. . . . The tree-leaves were knitted into laces to lay against the silver shine of moon, and all about, was the magic of silver and old lace. . . . A dazzling light, and queer things became discernible.

Nancy was no longer listening to Gerald's silly speeches. She was
thinking. . . . She had come upon "Some train of reflection which art
can seldom lead or skill assist; but which will reveal itself as great
truths have done, by chance." Idly, she began to pick out objects that
were distinguishable in the moonlight. It grew fascinating. And she
laughed aloud, when the luminous light dazzled her eyes into seeking awry. . . . She sought to share her fun with Gerald, who, somehow—silly little Nancy even remarked:—that Gerald was never
good company, unless he was playing at love. . . . He was an adept at
oogling and talking baby-talk. . . . But his oogles never included the
beggar down on the corner and cause him to drop a coin into the old
beggar's hat . . . as did John. . . . Nor did it ever include a wistful
child with his face pressed to the window of a candy-shop. Once they
had come across the Widow Green's boy, with his face glued to a
show-window. She remembered the child's expectant grin when he
caught the sound of her voice. . . . How eagerly he had wheeled
about, thinking to see John, and his disappointment—that was not
allayed—at sight of Gerald.

Nancy was thinking, at last. . . .

Gerald would not join her in the pastime though she went on
tripping along beside him, with her hand still lying upon his arm. . . .
She saw many, many things, some masquerading in the moonlight so
well, until she could not, try as she would, discover what they were:
others startlingly distinct.

They were alongside a yard, a homelike yard with a low picket
fence, that set jamb-up to the pavement. A paling clamped to the
fence, was one of the supports for a clothesline which swung across
the yard. A portion of the line was very near the walk and a wash had
been left out to sway and flap and swish in the breeze. . . . A pillow
slip bulged grotesquely and flapped and popped like a toy-pistol, and
swung limply waiting to be charged again with the soft night air.

Nancy's eyes swept the clothesline, then settled in a fixed stare at something there upon. . . .

At the same moment Gerald belched—he was quite near his destination. . . . "Moonlight is meant for lovers. . . ."

He was surprised out of all his smug niceties by the scream close under his ear that started to be shrill, then choked. . . . Nancy had snatched her hand from within the crook of his arm, before he could collect his scattered wits . . . and was fleeing like a mad thing back down the path they had come. . . . For an instant in his great astonishment, Gerald was struck by the beauty of that flight—a swift shadow vanishing in a silver mist—

But soon he was mumbling to himself, "What did she see? . . ."

"Ugh—," he shuddered. . . ."Ugh," he complained again. He was done with Nancy; wouldn't have no woman who could see things that-a-way. He muttered, stumbled, and continued on his way. . . .

While the night winds swayed the clothesline until it set to jerking, curiously, as if feet were in them kicking, a man's sox, cheap and coarse, even in the moonlight, and beside them dancing—the cream of silk and wool, pink at heel and toe; the finest they could buy—

An infant's tiny stockings. . . .

Indeed. . . . "There are chords in the human heart strange varying strings, which are only struck by accident. . . . Chords, which remain mute and senseless to appeals the most passionate and earnest—that respond at last, to the slightest, casual touch. . . ."

Messenger 8 (Aug. 1926): 229–231.

Unfinished Masterpieces

THERE ARE DAYS which stand out clearly like limpid pools beside the dusty road; when your thoughts, crystal clear as water, are pinioned in loveliness like star-points. Solitary days, which come often, if you are given to browsing in fields of past adventure; or rarely, if you are seldom retrospective; and not at all, if you are too greatly concerned with rushing onward to a nebulous future. Days whereupon your experiences glimmer before you waveringly like motion-pictures and the people you have known stroll through the lanes of memory, arrayed in vari-colored splendour or in amusing disarray. Days like these are to be revered, for they have their humors and their whimsicalities. Hurry your thoughts and the gathering imageries take flight. Perplexity but makes the lens of introspection blur. And of annoyance beware, for it is an evil vapour that disseminates and drowns the visions in the sea of grim realities. Such days must be cultivated. Scenes for their reception must be set. Cushions perhaps, and warmth of fire. Above all, the warmth of sweet content. Ease and comfort, comfort and ease and moods of receptivity. Then hither, come hither the places and the people we have known, the associations that withstand time's effacements. Backward ho, through the mazes of the past.

Stop! "Why howdy, Dora Johns." Darling playmate of my child-years. With wooly hair a length too short for even pigtails. Mud-spatters upon your funny black face. Mud-spatters all over your dress and your little black hands mud-spattered too.

Why? What? Come on and see. And lo! I am a child again.

Hand in hand, unmindful of her muddy ones, we skip around the old ramshackle house, back to the furthest corner of an unkempt yard, impervious to the tin cans, the ash-heap, the litter, the clutter that impedes our way, our eyes upon, our thoughts bent upon one small clean-swept corner, where there is mud. More mud and water in a battered tin can. And row after row of mud. No, not mud—not merely mud, but things made out of mud. Row on row, drying in the sun.

Carefully, I sit down, doubling up, to be as small as possible, for only this corner where mud things are drying is clean and corners are seldom, if ever, quite large enough. Besides, I must not touch the things made out of mud. If the dried ones fall, they break. If the moist ones are molested, be it with ever so gentle a finger, they lose their shape. Moreover, I must not disturb Dora.

Her little hands are busied with the mud. Little moulder's fingers are deftly playing their skill. Her child's face is alight. What has splashed her grave child's face with such a light? I wondered. I wonder now. The glitter of brittle talent, a gleam of sterling genius or the glow from artistic fires burning within the soul of a little black child?

Little Dora shaping figures out of mud. Vases and urns, dolls and toys, flying birds and trotting horses, frisking dogs and playing kittens, marvelous things out of mud. Crying aloud as though dealt a blow if one of the dried mud-figures is broken. Working in mud for endless hours, while the neighbor children play. Their hilarious merriment dropping like bombs into the quiet of our clean-swept corner. Deadly missiles seeking to find a mark. The insistent halloes of futile mirth forever bubbling on the other side of a high-board fence.

The dividing fence and upon one side the clean-swept corner and the row on row of mud things drying in the sun. And Dora seeming not to heed the seething bubbles upon the other side, shaping, shaping marvelous things out of mud.

Yet, oh Dora, now that the day is ours, will you not say, "When did the bombs of futile mirth strike their target? When did the tin-cans and the rags and the old ash-heap crowd you out from your clean-swept corner? What rude hand caused the dried mud shapes to fall and break? Who set a ruthless foot in the midst of your damp mud things?" Or were you too plastic, as plastic as your mud? You dare not tell. Only this you can whisper into the mists of our today. You are one of the Master's unfinished shapes which He will some day gather to mould anew into the finished masterpiece.

A lump of mud. Now, there is a sobriquet for you—you funny, funny man. Mr. William Williams. I saw you but once. We chanced to meet in the home of a mutual friend. I thought you so very funny then. Uncouth and very boorish, but ever, when these pageants of the past, these dumb shows of inarticulate folks arise before me upon retrospective days, you appear garbed in the tatters of pathos.

"I am fifty-one years old," you kept repeating. How pitiful those fifty-one years are. You wear a child's simplicity, the sort that is so sad to see upon a man. Fifty-one and penniless. Fifty-one and possessed of naught else but the clothing you wore. Fifty-one and no place on earth you might call home. You confessed to being a vagabond though "bum" was the term you used and you were very proud of your one accomplishment, an ability to avoid all labor.

"I've given no man a full day's honest work in all my fifty-one years," you boasted. "I gambles. I ain't no cotton-pickin' nigger." Your one and only boast after holding life, the fathomless fountain of eter-nal possibilities, in your possession for fifty-one priceless years.

Nevertheless you have lived and so intensely. You held us against our will. Clustered around you, listening to you talk. Relating clip-pings as it were from the scrap-book of your life.

Tales of the road, of the only places you knew. Roads leading away from plantations where the cotton waited to be picked by number-less "cotton-pickin' niggers." Roads leading to pool halls and gambling dens. Roads beginning and roads ending in "riding the roads," carrying backward and forward, here and yon through the weird goblin land of the South's black belt.

With a hardened casualness you told stories that revolted and at the same time cheered us with an all sufficing glow of thankfulness that life had spared us the sordidness of yours. Offhandily, you gave us humourous skits that tempered our laughter with wishes that we might know at least a bit of such a droll existence as had been yours. With magical words you painted pictures so sharply they cut scars upon our hearts. You drew others so filled with rollicking delight their gladsomeness was contagious. With the nonchalance of a player shuffling cards you flipped your characters before us, drawn directly from the cesspool of your contacts, and spellbound we listened.

Someone remarked how wonderful you talked and you replied, "Once, I sorter wanted to write books. Once, I uster read a heaps. See times when I was broke and nobody would stake me for a game, I'd lay around and read. I've read the Bible through and through and every *Police Gazette* I could lay my hands on. Yes, suh, I've read a heap. And I've wished a lot'er times I'd sense enough to write a book."

Lump of mud. Containing the you, the splendid artist in you, the soul of you, the unfinished you in the ungainly lump of you, awaiting the gathering-up to be moulded anew into the finished masterpiece.

What a day! Here is my friend at whose fire-side I have lingered beholding Mr. William Williams, great lump of mud. To be sure, she also is an unfinished production. Though it is apparent that the Master had all but done when she slipped from his hands and dropped to earth to lie groping like the rest of us thereon.

Let us sit here together, friend, and enjoy this day.

I shall try to discover what recent gift you have given to the poor the while you are quietly stitching upon the garments, linens and scarlet, with which to clothe your household. Sit here and smile with the welcoming light in your eyes, knowing that your door is open to such as William Williams and Dora Johns, the Dora who is become as the mud beneath one's feet. Kind mistress of the widely opened door where white and black, rich and poor, of whatever caste or creed may enter and find comfort and ease and food and drink.

Let me sit awhile beside you upon this day, hearkening again to your simple philosophy. A philosophy stirred with the spoon of kindliness and seasoned with the essence of love. Very simple indeed and yet sufficient to sustain you in every trial and of such resilience it rebounds in the presence of tribulations unto itself and findeth peace.

What is it you say to back-biters and gossips, all those who wrongfully accuse you? "Everything will come out in the wash."

And when a haughty one is being superior? "Birds fly high but they come down to get water."

And when something or someone has failed you in duty or in word? "Every tub has to stand on its own bottom."

And your simple panacea for intolerance? "Man is 'apt' to fall as sparks go upwards."

What boon would I not forswear to sit beside you in reality, my friend, who boasts no art save the art of friendliness?

Friendliness encased in a crust of black mud, awaiting also the Master's final touch, when all outer semblances and material hindrances shall fade into nothingness and His gifts, be they the one talent or the five, shall be poured into His scales.

So thinking, retrospection suddenly done with, retracing with leaps and bounds the journey through the fields of memory, I arrive at the stile of the present. Whereon there is a sign as vividly lined as the present is drawn from the past and future from the present. Quite plainly it reads:

"We one and all are God's unfinished shapes, ungainly lumps of mud, waiting—waiting to be moulded anew into the finished masterpiece."

Crisis 34 (March 1927): 14, 24–25.

"G'long, Old White Man's Gal . . ."

"WHAT YOU-ALLS RECKON . . . what you-alls reckon, now?" old Nancy Little, shriveled and black as an aged prune, had just entered Newman's drug store. Newman, himself, lolled against one of his counters and superintended the black "Sheik" of a fellow in clean white coat and apron who waited to serve Newman's customers. Couples were grouped around two of the little tables. A dark-eyed yellow Miss with her "company," a big shining black lout, were perched on high stools at the soda fountain.

Old Nancy looked over her audience gloatingly. She was so little and thin that one wondered what had consumed her. Having attracted the attention of her audience, she walked over to the waiting sheik and mumblingly requested a fifty-cent box of stuff. This done she again inquired in her crackled old voice, "What you-alls reckon?"

The audience, there was always one to be had at Newman's, obligingly shook its head and discreetly assimilated keen interest. They knew old Nancy.

"Well, I tells you-all," Old Nancy spoke tantalizingly slow. "Some ol' white man's done willed that thar Mercy

Kent ah fortune." Envy. It was so patent in her manner that one decided it was envy and envy alone that had eaten her up.

Silence ensued, a murky, smudgy silence in which evil thoughts could breed.

After a while, Newman, himself, condescended from his state of surveying boss to the extent of pooh-poohing old Nancy's statement. She wheeled on him like a startled cat, saying with vehement conviction, "I was right thar when the news come. She's got a legacy I tells you-all. Some ol' white man's named her in his will 'n' everythin', and beque'thed Mercy Kent a good sized fortune."

"Uhuh, now what'd I tell yuh?" exclaimed the yellow Miss at the soda fountain.

"Pshaw," laughed her escort sneeringly, "Don't you 'spect I allus knowed it?"

"A leegacy?" inquired one from among the group at a table. "Say, sister, couldn't yuh be mistaken?"

"Humph! Don't you-alls start that, young feller; whatever ol' Nancy talks 'bout she's either heerd it, see'd it, or smelt it. Ain't I done told you-alls I was thar when the news come?" Here old Nancy dropped her belligerence and spoke confidingly, "Those fool Kents were so brazen they just lets me hear all on it. Some ol' man or nuther named Endlidge—Mr. Endlidge, Mr. Endlidge you-alls understand done paid you-alls high filutin' Miss Mercee Kent for a lots she's done, I reckon. Now you-alls can take it or leave it. I done told what I knows. And if it's a lie, you-all hear me, the mail what the postman brought and the envelope and read right fore these here eyes and the words what these here ears of mine heerd, they's all done lied too."

Old Nancy took up her small packet from off the counter and dropped her fifty cent piece down with a clatter. She hobbled towards the door, then turned and came back. She was like a little black spider in the midst of them, weaving a web with which to catch flies. And the flies, see them, flies will always be caught. "Listen here, them

Kents never let us know when this here started now it ain't for us to be runnin' after them when the things ended. I reckons you-all know no white man's ain't ever left no black gal somethin' for nuthin'."

At old Nancy's departure the remaining coterie drew closer together.

"Whats I allus told yuh," were the words most rampant. At last, so they surmised, they had the clue to Mercy Kent's high-hat manners.

"Oh no, she don't go with nobody. Oh no, oh no." All but chanted a slim youth who had been one of the many who felt it was worth Mercy's while to pay attention to himself.

"Deed, ain't this rich? But I allus suspected some such," drawled another.

"Oh brother, little pussy-cat done jumped out the bag."

"It's some reason for being so high and mighty, I'll say."

"It's your high sailing kite what gits tangled up in the telegraph wires."

"That's cold, feller, nuthing but bombs explode."

"Go way, Bud, this here is one of Lindy's planes that's gone and punctured her wings."

"Say, I heard th' crash."

"Didja?"

Old Nancy hobbled along with unwonted speed. Soon she reached Brothels, the green grocers'. Pete Brothel the proprietor was a fat, pig-eyed, greasy, salacious gentleman of color. He hailed Nancy's gossip with loud-mouthed laughter that made his fat shoulders billow and shake. "Well yes," he ejaculated, "well yes."

"So the bile's busted right in th' ol' hen . . . well yes." He leaned far over a fruit stall to wag a pudgy finger in old Nancy's face, then he winked an eye meaningly and slipped a slobbery tongue around his lips by way of preparing for further discourse. A necessary but an inopportune and transient customer came in, whereupon old Nancy having other places to go darted out, grimacing with unctuous satisfaction as she went for she knew that greasy Pete would do his bit towards spreading the gossip after his own fashion.

The Kents were not popular among their neighbors, for Welsh Street demanded free and easy manners of all its habitues. It welcomed display; it encouraged ostentation; it lauded opulence; but it fully and decidedly resented and denounced what it called, "Airs."

Long since, the Welsh Streeters had attached "airs" to the name of Kents. The Kents lived in the white and green cottage at the end of the street. White and green, mind you, when all the other nondescript houses on Welsh were drab greys and ugly duns. There were many grievances against them such as screened doors and windows and of all unheard-of airs, a screened-in back porch. Neat flower beds in their front yard, and not a single scraggly chicken to peck a livelihood at their back door, and when all the neighborhood youngsters had wallowed at will in the dusty street the Kent young one in stiffly starched gingham and ribbon bows in her hair had spent her time among the flower beds, playing "a leery" with her rubber ball or mimicking grown-ups with her dolls and china tea-set. Or "airs" untold, Sarah Kent, mother, the unpardonably guilty one with her "yaller" face and straight hair had taken the small though albeit stout and stumpy Mercy by the hand and gone off walking, strutting scandalously down the length of Welsh Street, looking neither to the right or to the left but dividing her attention between her small daughter who clung to one hand and to the gay red parasol which she held carefully over herself with the other.

The neighbors said it was because she feared black; they joshed each other about it, and declared that they could mark the seasons by watching Sarah Kent for all summer long, the red parasol, and when the shrill winds blew, Sarah left off the parasol and adopted veils to shield her complexion.

When grown older, Mercy went off to school, and upon her return the Welsh Street youths had never quite dared to approach her. True, they delighted to group themselves on the corner and look her over. The more intrepid ones made remarks at ear-shot distance, but something in Mercy's manner piqued them. They couldn't say that she did not notice them, because she did. She looked at them impersonally from wide-set eyes with a cool tolerant stare that ruffled them amazedly, nor could they explain just how she made them feel except by shrug of shoulder and disgruntled "humph."

Old John Kent, father, had been employed up town for a great many years—"'snooping' 'round Buckram white folks," Welsh Street said. How-be-it, he earned enough to foot the bills for all the "'airs'" his folks put on. He had grown old in the performance of simple service; he had aided any fellow-man who needed his assistance. To him, it had seemed neither strange or unfitting to reach out a helping hand to Pat Endlidge when Endlidge, a white man, had slumped beneath successive loads of hard-luck. He had considered Endlidge's fervent promises to pay back double fold just so much chaff threshed out from his field of fertile service. Moreover, as for being paid, old Kent imagined that his white and green cottage, his flower-beds, and his women-folk were recompense enough for anything he had ever done or might ever do. To partake of one of Sarah's dinners after a hard day's work; to sit back, deep in his old arm-chair, listening to Mercy's tinkling touch upon the piano keys. He had long thought that he wished for nothing else.

Then like a long-in-coming boomerang, a letter bringing the information that Patrick Endlidge after twenty-five years had kept his promise. It was something to thank God for and to be proud of. It proved many things which had smouldered down in the red glow of kindliness in old Kent's heart:—that now and then, white folks did remember the hand that fed. . . . that bread cast on the water does come back. . . . that the righteous—not that he set himself up as being so righteous, but he tried to be—was never forsaken and his seed would never beg.

"God a' mighty, God a' mighty. . . . Now Mercy need not beg!" Like a revelation it came to him, that all along he had wanted money,

money, money, that all along he had been worrying over what he was going to leave behind for Mercy. He thought with warming chuckles of delight how Patrick Endlidge had put one over on him, repaid home one thousand-fold. A gift to himself would have been all right, but no, old Endlidge, the crook, had reached further than that. He had given to Mercy, his child, his little old gal, his Mercy.

There was rejoicing within the little white and green cottage, the sort of joy that bubbles over the rim and splashes down the sides, and makes little puddles about the bottom of the bucket and eventually forms into little rivulets to run here and there and everywhere.

The Kents thought gleefully that it had been propitious that old Nancy the neighborhood gossip had been there to share their news. They wondered in innocent merriment what folks would say. . . .

Sarah who had secretly bemoaned that her daughter Mercy at twenty-eight was yet unmarried, immediately re-lit her hopes. Money—how sweet the thought—would conceal her daughter's shortcomings like smoke does flame. Who would care now, that Miss Mercy Kent was a roly-poly, that her features were blunt, and her complexion swart or that her none too luxuriant hair was stubby and kinky, and that Mercy for all her usual good-nature was too stubborn or too lazy—Sarah could not decide which—to resort to cosmetics or to submit to the hair-dresser's art of pressing her crinkly locks into rigid straightness.

From the instant that she knew of her "luck" Mercy had been in a dream, a veritable daze of pleasure that enwrapped her. To think of having more money than she had ever imagined. To think she could go places, some place, maybe, that would be more friendlier towards her than Welsh Street. Yes, they would all go, go somewhere and start over. No. That could not be; it would break her parents' heart to pull up and leave this spot of their choice. It was funny, she thought, how black people became rooted to the soil like stumps, and besides, her father and mother were old, so old, they did not sense their neighbor's hostility or perhaps they had grown hardened to it. Leastway, they did not mind the ostracism which Welsh Street levelled upon them. Although—her sudden good fortune was softening her heart—perhaps she herself was too critical of Welsh Street. She would stay, that's what she would, among these people whom she had always known. Stay among them and spend her wealth with them and on them and for them. They were her people, she too was a stump rooted in this soil.

Unnoticed by either Sarah or John, she slipped out of the house. She wanted to walk, an urge beset her to wander among the old familiar surroundings of Welsh Street with its ramshackle houses, and its wallowing youngsters, and its idling youths, and its loitering grown-ups. She went briskly in the rolling gait that was hers. Her heavy breasts jostling with each step, her hips rippling beneath the folds of her skirt, her trim ankles and small feet catching the eye almost forcibly. Though she was unaware of it, her head sat at a haughty angle, and bobbed slightly as she walked as the head of a spirited horse does.

She was thinking about the money that would be hers, when some unkempt youngsters suddenly sprang up before her and scudded away. She laughed at their sudden flight, never once suspecting that she was the cause of it, and instantly decided that it would be nice to use some of her legacy to build a play-ground for the youngsters on Welsh Street. Supposing, so ran her thoughts, she would take in that vacant lot out by Simmons, and fix it up, swings, and slides, and. . . .

Of a sudden, she was aware of Newman's, and as usual, it swarmed with black folk. A victrola screeched "blues." Mercy could see into the store and across to the soda-fountain as she approached. Two couples sat before the counter smirking at her disdainfully. As she drew in front of the entrance, a slim black youth in spotless attire sauntered out, rudely crossing before her, and without lifting his cap, he met her eye fully, and spat.

Above the waves of laughter that rushed at her, loud words struck her, sinking like lead in deep water, down, down, into her heart . . . "G'long ol' white man's gal."

Instinctively, Mercy's chin lifted, and her head bobbed a trifle faster, the rippling of her hips beneath her skirts became a bit more marked just for the interval of her passage before Newman's. Then, as she reached the corner, she staggered like a wounded beast, fighting to stand on her feet, fought desperately, before plunging headlong down the street for the haven of a white and green cottage.

Messenger 10 (April 1928): 81–82.

"White Folks's Nigger"

WELSH STREET ADORED PAGEANTRY of any sort, but it relished above all, the doleful pompishness of funerals. Let there be a funeral, and a crowd was assured, for "the last sad rites" fed an insatiable hunger which lay deep within the beings of the Welsh Street people. But despite their usual prodigious attendance at all obsequies, the numbers that thronged to witness the service for old Uncle Dickson actually out-did itself.

Not only was Welsh Street disturbed at this funeral but the region beyond Welsh was involved, and for the nonce, the line of demarcation was wrenched asunder, all but uprooted. At a time, too long ago to remember, old Uncle Dickson burst the confining bonds of his surroundings, and went to live with white folks. Now, he, old white-folks's-nigger-Dickson, was dead. And the Balsams, the whites with whom he had lived, had brought him back to Welsh Street for burial.

"Weren't good 'nough to be buried 'mongst white folks, huh. Weren't fit to have no service for him in no white chu'ch." For in Welsh Street none believed the glib tongued white man, one of the younger Balsams, who got up in Mount Olive, the colored church with the largest membership, and announced the passing of "great old Uncle Dick." "It was," so he spoke, "out of respects to his memory that they were bringing him back to his own people to be laid to rest."

The funeral was to be Tuesday. And the young white man had allowed how pleased he knew old Dick would be to have everybody come to the service. "Tet, tet," tongues were thrust into cheeks as young Balsam sat down. "Bringing him back, tell it Mister, for good riddance. . . . You all don't want old-nigger-Dick clutterin' up you-all's grave yard. 'Cause the old fool can't work no more."

As it were, the service was not held in any church. Old Uncle Dickson had never been converted. He had never professed any religion, and therefore he could not look for peace in death or hope for redemption at the judgment. Such a death as his was a fire-brand to throw in the midst of sinners. It was an opportunity that had to be used, so the pious ones, the staunch old members of every church in Welsh Street, came forward and refused to allow the body of this "dead-and-done-for-sinner" to be brought into the church.

However, old Uncle Dickson was a lodge member in good standing. Throughout the thirty years that he had spent on alien soil, he had trudged dutifully back to Welsh Street, twice a month, to attend meetings. And the doors of the Masonic hall were thrown open for the service to be held there.

Tuesday came, and all preparations for old Uncle Dick's funeral had been made. Since one o'clock that afternoon, Welsh Street had been like a spreading fan. Men in solemn black, and women, in complacent disregard for solemnity, decked in clashing hues of every known shade and coloring, and children in wide-eyed, Sabbath-day splendor poured down the flutes of the fan and disappeared as though with the closing of the fan into Masonic hall.

The first arrivals from Welsh Street found something there. That which had brought them, drawn them, as a magnet does steel, death, lay in the long coffin that stretched across the isle diffusing an icy breath. The oppressiveness of the stillness of death hung over everything. However, having lured them here from far and wide, from every nook and corner of Welsh Street, death straightway lost its power to attract. Life claimed the living, and white eyes in dark faces widened with expectation of receiving some scant meal of excitement from life. Suddenly, sobs long and stifled uttered by someone exhausted with crying, beat into the stillness. Instantly, all were alert. Certainly, no such demonstration of grief had been looked for, for who should weep for old-white-folks's-nigger-Dickson? Necks were craned, and eyes searched. Who could the mourner be? Discovery followed closely, "Huh, that there white girl."

Whites were there in plenty. Friends of the Balsams, they were, and inconvertly, Uncle Dick's friends, too. As if an unseen cordon had been drawn, the blacks drew to one side of the house, the whites to the other, until with the impact of many bodies a dividing line was made as neatly as though with a surgeon's knife. While up in front, old Dickson, rigid in the chill embrace of death, lay in his coffin which stretched in almost equal proportions on either side of the separating space, as though testifying to the leveling hands of death. Even now, the whites and blacks were mingling in a closer bond than could have been permissable upon any other occasion.

None expected the air of hushed bereavement which fell upon them after entering the hall. The sobbing, stifled and prolonged, made it seem so; it was alive with grief. And they came racking from the delicate throat of the sixteen year old daughter of the house, the most prized and the best tended shoot of the Balsam tree.

After the first startled glances, the whites began to whisper one to the other. "He nursed her from her infancy," they said. "He was as faithful as an old dog," they murmured. "Though really, I think, her mother should have prevented such an attachment," they emphasized. "The child hasn't an iota of self-restraint, it's disgusting," they criticized. Having made their remarks, the whites retreated within themselves like turtles into their shells, and sat bolt upright in their places, staring.

The blacks grew self-conscious. Disgust and satisfaction—hops and sugar—seemed to swell them up. "Humph," their unspoken grunts permeated the silence that was broken only by terrible sobs. "Took care of her since the day she was born. Given her every single thing he could beg, borrow, or steal. Forsaken everbody he'd ever known for them white folks. 'Deed they oughter spill some tears. I 'spects though, they's thinking 'bout nothing but the work he can't do no more." Wooly heads shaken dolefully bespoke derision far more than sorrow.

When it appeared that no more people could possibly enter the hall, the service began. A fat black man arose ponderously and stood up in front, but by no means beside the coffin, that and what lay within it was an example. The discourse which he was about to deliver would prove with finality the bitter end of all sinners. He lifted his plump fat hands, and spread out his fingers as one about to play the pianoforte. He grimaced; he opened his mouth wide; he pursed his lips; after which he opened his mouth as wide as he could, which was not a little, then drew his lips together to that degree which allowed his voice to issue forth in sputtering tones. Sputteringly, he read from the Scriptures:

"Go ye into all the world and preach the gospel to every creature. He that believeth and be baptized shall be saved, but he that believeth not shall be damned." Closing his book with a thud, he smacked his lips, spread his fingers, pivoted upon his toes, clasped his hands before him, and stood for a moment looking towards Elinor Balsam whose sobbing made a hollow accompaniment for his words.

Even though every eye was upon him, his utterance sputtered forth unexpectantly; he launched into it without any further preliminaries:

"Brothers and sisters, death, the grim old reaper, done laid our friend and brother, Amos Dickson, low, so low. He's dead; brothers and sisters, he's dead. Yes indeed, he's dead now, but God done let him stand 'til hoar frost done covered his head. 'Til old-man-wrinkles done covered his face. 'Til the winds of sorrow and the storms of trials done give him a stoop. . . . Now brothers and sisters, what you-alls reckon God done let him stand for, yes sir, stand up all these long years, right up on his two feet, what you-all reckons God done let him stand up for?" He paused for a second or more, gazing earnestly into the uplifted faces before him.

Reverend "Ah Lords" greeted his questioning.

"Brothers and sisters," resumed the speaker, "I don't needs to ask you what God done let him stand here so long for. The Christians in this here house, knows, and the sinners needs to find out. I wish I could stand up here before you-alls and say that our brother Amos Dickson has gone to meet my Jesus. But, oh Lord, oh Lord, oh Lord, I can't." He chanted dolorously while casting curious white-eyed glances at his white audience. "Brothers and sisters," he took up his discourse in confidential tones, "let me tells you, if you make your bed in hell, you got'er lay there. Now we alls know that this sinner man never took time to find Jesus." Loud fervent intonations of "Have mercy muy Jesus" drowned out his voice. He waited patiently while the noise subsided. Resuming his speech in a yet more intimate way, he continued: "Did this sinner man ever get himself buried in the liquid grave? I'm just asking you Christians so these here sinner folks in this house can hear me." He announced with dramatic emphasis, and deliberately leaned his weight against the wall and waited. No other sound was made save Elinor Balsam's sobbing. The Negroes began to sway as the silence grew into minutes, and presently mumbling voices calling upon the Lord for mercy fluttered upwards, to surround the preacher with the desired atmosphere.

Suddenly he swayed away from the supporting wall and shouted in a great booming voice that no longer spluttered. "Then I wants to know, brothers and sisters, how's he going to be saved? This sinner man what use'ter be our friend and our brother ain't with us no more, and he ain't with the Lord. He's with that old man, the devil, who's always a-hankerin' for sinners to come live with him. Let me tells you sinners what's in this here house under the sound of my voice, if you don't hurry and join the band here on earth, you sure won't get no chance to join it in heaven. Yes, indeed, you-alls will be footloose like you-alls craves to be, but you will be footloose in hell.

I reckon, sinners don't ever stop to study 'bout the red hot rods that's down there waiting to lash 'em, and the red ashes what's waiting to make 'em a bed, and the boiling fish-oil what's waiting for 'em to drink. I guess they don't study 'bout it not being no bread down there for 'em to eat, nothing but red hot cinders." Changing his loud harsh tones suddenly into a prayerful plea spoken in a minor key he exhorted, "Oh Lord, oh Lord, have mercy on poor Amos Dickson down there in all that fiery discord. Dear Jesus do go down there and blow your breath on him, speak to him, dear Jesus, and tell him you done give him a chance to be saved. Blessed Jesus save the sinners in this house, speak to 'em Lord and make 'em see what you done to our poor departed brother—"

Loud moans and voices crying, "Have mercy Lord," completely drowned the preacher's closing remarks. And like a throbbing minor note, Elinor Balsam's weeping sounded above the devout cries. Suddenly the Negro voice dissolved into a hymn:

> *Oh my lovin' brother don't you*
> *want God's bosom*
> *To be your pillow when the world's*
> *on fire-ah.*

Slowly the song died away. After a moment of inaction another man, young and sombre-eyed, apparently a minister also, got up and took the place of the previous speaker, but standing nearer the coffin, in fact so close to it that he could press down one of his slim brown hands against the shining surface of the casket. Elinor Balsam's sobs affected him visibly. Sympathy softened his dark, grave face. As he stood there quietly in front of the large and mixed audience death's icy breath grew warmer, Elinor's sobs beat down into little long-drawn gasps. Not a soul stirred; every eye was upon him.

Slowly, he began, repeating words that seemed to have but then dawned upon him, bringing to him a new and clearer meaning. "Whosoever will be chief among you, let him be your servant."

The rustle of stiffening backs drawn upright against hard seats settled into quiet before he spoke again.

"I see hands," he announced with a startling vividness. "Old, old hands, wrinkled, toil-worn hands, extended in supplication to the Christ. Such hands . . . stained and roughened with service and withal so tender, gentle, and kind. Look at them, friend, look at those hands, and tell me is there any one of you who can believe that these hands are raised to the savior in vain." Never once had he raised his voice: it was fraught with sincerity.

Softly fell Elinor Balsam's tears like healing balm for her sorrowing heart. Silently the young minister stood firm footed upon this old, but ever new, doctrine which he had flung into the faces of his hearers, and one slender brown hand pressed the shining surface of Uncle Dickson's coffin.

Spontaneously, with an instinctive knowledge of what is fitting, the Negroes were singing,

> *There's plenty good room*
> *There's plenty good room*
> *A way in the kingdom*
> *There's plenty good room.*

Messenger 10 (May–June 1928): 104, 111, 114, 117, 119.

Cross Crossings Cautiously

Sᴀᴍ Tɪᴍᴏɴs rarely thought in the abstract. His thoughts as were his affections were marshaled concretely. His affections were rolled into a compact and unbreakable ball which encircled his wife Lettie and his young son Sammy. His thoughts—he did not think much—but such as his thoughts were, they involved this, if he did a good turn for somebody, somebody else would quite naturally do him or his a good turn also.

Usually Sam was a cheerful creature. Work and love; love and work, that, boiled down to brass tacks is the gist of all life, and Sam possessed both. Even though, at present, he was out of a job.

He walked along the sandy road stirring up miniature dust clouds with every step for his heavy feet shuffled wearily with the burden of his dejected body.

He felt down and out. He was at the end of his rope. One dollar in his pocket. He gripped it in his fingers. All he had. But he could not give up. The ball of his affection, as it were, trundled along before him luring him on. He was "hoofing it" to another town to try again.

"Saw wood . . . clean house, paint barns, chop weeds . . . plow, anything, suh. . . . Just so it's work so's I can earn somethin'. I'm a welder by trade, but they don't hire cullud."

Behind him stretched the long, dusty way he had come. Before him a railroad zigzagged his path. As his feet lifted to the incline, he raised his eyes, and met advice from a railroad crossing sign:

CROSS CROSSINGS CAUTIOUSLY

He paused to spell out the words, repeating them painstakingly. Then he went on. A little beyond and across the tracks another huge sign caught his attention.

Soon, he had halted beside this one, letting his eyes sidle up and down and over the gaily painted board. Now he was staring open-mouthed at the glaring yellow lion who crouched to spring, now, at the flashy blond lady pirouetting on a snow white mount. He stood quite still thinking. Wouldn't Lettie and little Sam be wild to see such a show.

"'Lo Mister."

Sam swung around like a heavy plummet loosed from its mooring.

"Gee . . . Mister, you 'fraid of me?"

A little girl hardly more than a baby addressed him. She was regarding him with the straight unabashed gaze of the very innocent and of the very wise.

"I want you to carry me to the circus," she announced, when their mutual survey of one another seemed to her enough.

Sam's eyes were fixed on the web-fine, golden hair escaping from two torn places in the child's hat. Already he had seen that the eyes searching his were blue. . . . He fidgeted. He made a move to go.

"Oh, don't, don't go," beseeched the child. "Mother has to 'tend a meeting, and father is always busy. There is no one else. Mother said

I might if only somebody'd take me. See." She thrust out a little smudgy fist—and opening it, revealed a shiny new fifty-cent piece. "This is mine," she said plaintively, "can't we go?"

⚐⚑

MRS. MAXIMUS McMARR was a busy woman. She managed to attend fourteen clubs each week, but that excluded any time to manage Claudia, her five-year-old daughter. Claudia's father considered children woman's responsibility. One advantage or disadvantage this sort of bringing up gave Claudia, she always got what she wanted.

Something about her made Sam do her bidding now.

They were half way between the McMarr place and the circus grounds before he thought about what he was doing. He clutched at the dollar in his pocket. He wanted to laugh, guessed he was nervous. Suddenly, he stopped abruptly—there was another of those signs where the train's right-of-way intersected another dusty country road.

CROSS CROSSINGS CAUTIOUSLY

"Oh do come on," urged the child jerking his hand in an ecstasy of delight and impatience.

Further on a half-grown lad passed them, but stopped and turned to watch them down the road. As the man and the little girl drew out of sight, he faced about and pelted up the road.

The noise of the circus leapt up to meet and welcome Sam and Claudia. The music of the band was sweet to their ears. Sam reveled in it and Claudia's little feet danced over the road. Even the bellowing and roars of the wild animals left them undismayed. It was circus day.

Mrs. McMarr had alighted from a friend's car and remained standing beside it, to talk. Both women observed the runner at the same time. Mrs. McMarr felt her heart skid upward into her throat. Claudia had not appeared. She divined that the messenger tended evil for no other than her precious baby. She made up her mind to swoon even before she received the tidings.

The friend went in search of McMarr who for once allowed himself an interruption. Close-lipped, he tumbled off his harvester and rushed pell-mell across his field.

All afternoon, Claudia had been surfeited with care. One after another had tendered and petted and caressed her. Even her father had been solicitous. She curled up, drowsy and very tired, in the big arm chair.

The rain that had threatened to fall all day suddenly commenced like the tat-a-rat-tat of far-off drums. Claudia was wide awake. She sat up. Remembering. The circus band! The monkeys in their little red coats! Her circus man! Something had happened. What?

The impulse to know surmounted the fear she harbored of her father. She slipped over to his chair. He had been very kind today. Perhaps . . . he wouldn't mind telling her . . . Where her circus man was?

Opportunity 8 (June 1930): 177, 189.

The Eternal Quest

WHEN EVAN GIVEN gave up his wife to that grim reaper who holds a mortgage on every man's house and forecloses with or without notice, he turned with a stolid, white-hot passion to his baby, a year-old daughter, for what little comfort he could squeeze from life. The love that he severed with such visible effort from the mother to bestow upon the offspring doubled and trebled in the years during which Polly Given grew up.

At eighteen, she was a sweet flower of a girl. Then, as stealthily as comes the dew at even-tide, the Reaper struck again, deftly, swiftly, and Polly sped forth into the unknown whither Evan dared not follow. And the reason that he dared not was because of a tiny spark that glowed in the very depth of his being—his faith. He believed in life after death, and that the self-destroyer forfeited much if not all of the future existence.

Because Evan Given was one of the foremost surgeons of his day, and dabbled in science as a side-line, it was not altogether incredible, after his burdensome grief, that he elected to give up the one in which he had won fame and fortune for the other, the lesser as a buffer for his sorrow. Quietly, and with no more ado than is usual for a man changing his barber, he dropped all else, and took up the study of science—the science of faith. He closed his house, the palatial dwelling, he had erected for his daughter; cut his London connections, and set himself adrift, as much as it was possible for a man of his standing to do.

What is this thing, faith. . . . Why does it suffice for some. . . . Why is it insufficient for others. . . . Why believing as I do that God is the giver, and therefore has a Divine right to take when and as He wills, am I rebellious because he has bereft me of mine? These were the questions Evan Given sought to solve.

No. 60 in ward 400 was one of the strangest cases ever admitted to the county hospital. His was a unique malady and of a far-reaching scope. Plainly it came under the category of cases wherein the great Evan Given had labored so magnificently. It was known that the famous English surgeon was sojourning in the American city. If he could be prevailed upon to grant but an hour of his time, if for no more than a consultation, if only for an observation, anything he might choose to do would be a priceless gift to the medical profession.

At last, when all arguments had failed, someone mentioned that, which seemed to him, the strangest phase of the case in question, that this great hulking giant of a fellow—No. 60 was well over forty—should lay day after day, calling for his mother.

"That," said Evan Given, instantly, "is faith. Wait. I will come."

The span of No. 60's shoulders came near to over-taxing the width of the white iron cot. His massive head pressed against the head-post. His feet protruded through the foot rails. He was easily six foot ten, and he was delirious when Evan Given saw him first. He was strapped, but yet the strong thongs were proving inadequate, the motions of the man lifted the cot until it tossed about like a frail craft on a windy sea. And always, he screeched the one word, "mom-mer."

"Too late. . . . Nothing can be done!" proclaimed the great man. "At least, he can be made comfortable. Send for his mother!"

"There can be no visitors." Head Nurse of ward 400 voiced a protest, that was curbed at a glance from the Surgeon.

No. 60's mother arrived when he was at his worst. It was the crucial hour. He was seeking with maniacal strength to break his bonds, and screaming fiendishly. The mother, after a brief period with the great London physician, hurried to her son's bedside.

She was a small woman, a tightly shriveled, hard little person, not unlike a black walnut. . . . Her timidity fell from her, as she drew near the bed. She became no longer an uneasy visitor among countless strangers, but a mother with her only son, and it was he and she against the world.

The great Evan Given was a close observer of all that passed. This was a pregnant moment to him, in his study of faith.

The mother said quickly and a little shrilly, "Lie down 'dar." Then in firmer tones, and quieter: "Be still. Didn't ah tells you!"

Magically, the huge form upon the bed grew calm.

"What's you a-laying here fo', disturbin' these yere folks, ain't yo mammy done taught yo better'n 'at. . . ." Her voice was crooning.

"Ain't yo' shame yo'self. Here's yo mammy done come this long ways to see yo, and yo is lying here yellin' like yo is possessed."

"Mommer. . . ."

To the amazement of those watching, the man on the bed was muttering in his turn to the old woman. The mother down on her knees bent her head to hear. Quickly, she stood erect, and called loudly.

"Nurse . . . Doctor . . . somebody come quick and take off dese bindings. My boy wants to die free. . . . Come quick, somebody, quick."

Evan Given came—interns and nurses together removed the straps. No. 60 heaved a great sigh of relief. His head jerked back convulsively, and his eyes rolled wildly towards his mother. "De Lord's done come," he intoned majestically, and fell into his final sleep, peacefully as a babe.

"Faith," jotted Given, mentally.

The old woman sat beside the cot with folded hands. Evan cleared his throat. Surely this was a strange manner in which to meet death, not a tear, in no wise, did she betray regret. "Why-er—why-er," began Evan.

"Blessed lamb. . . . Sweet Jesus, done come and set my po' suf-f'ring boy, free," chanted the old woman, almost gaily.

"Faith," tabulated Given in his scientific mind.

"What will you do?" he inquired curiously, and not unkindly.

"Do heah this man," exclaimed No. 60's mother, "I's goin'er do muy wo'k." As an after-thought, "I'se got'er wo'k for sho' now, 'cause dis boy a-lying heah is my sole suppo't. But de Lord will provide."

"Faith," said Evan Given audibly in the voice of a man who talks often to himself. "I must find it."

Opportunity 9 (Aug. 1931): 242–243.

Two Old Women A-Shopping Go!

A Story of Man, Marriage and Poverty

WITHOUT A DOUBT, Nell had Horace on her mind. There was no forgetting the way he had pleaded with her, the night before. She had fallen to sleep thinking of him, not as on other nights when imagery made vivid by love, brought his dear presence near in her last wakeful moments to drift pleasantly through her dreams. No, not that way, but an unhappy picture of him, nervous and moody, penetrated her sleep and leaped to aliveness with her first wakefulness.

She remembered every word he had said, unfair, cruel words; now they formed crookedly and apart like bits of a jig-saw puzzle as she dressed. His arguments repeated themselves:

"Each day, we are growing older—"

Nell leaned nearer the mirror, and scanned her piquant face. Could it be that she really was aging and losing her charm, as surely as yesterday's flowers that drooped beside her in their squat, brown jar? A tiny line brought Nell's brows, silky, high-arched brows like the sweep of bird wings, together. She brushed her hair with brisk strokes, while thinking dejectedly:

"You will be old and grey."

Sudden panic seized her; she would not look for grey strands; no, not yet. She was not old, and she would not allow Horace to hurry her, frighten her into marrying him.

She put on her hat, a little round crocheted affair that she had made herself. She put on her coat and drew on her gloves, picked up her bag, and went out, an altogether lovely colored girl.

Nell thought how many mornings had she gone out, thus. Five years and every morning except Sundays, she had taken this same way: three steps down the cobble-stoned walk to the green latticed gate; half a block to the corner, turn North; four blocks to the car-line; a wait five or more minutes for the car; an hour's ride to work.

Last night, Horace had said, pleadingly . . .

"You'll be worn out, all fagged-to-death and, I—I—don't want the girl I marry worked to death before I get her."

Nell tried to brush her troublesome thoughts aside and quickened her steps, then as quickly found herself agreeing with Horace. She was tired, so tired. Unconsciously, the line that drew her lovely brows together, deepened.

She heard voices, and looking up, she saw two old women come trundling towards her.

One was a very black and very stout old lady buttoned to the throat in a long black coat that fitted tightly about the waist and bulged loosely about the hips. She carried a basket on her arm.

One was a very stout and white old lady with near-white-folk's hair straggling from beneath a brown bonnet. She was buttoned into a red knitted sweater. She wore a heavy worsted skirt, and over that, a white, starched apron that tied around her waist. She carried a black shopping-bag in her hand.

Thought Nell: two old ladies out to do their shopping. Making a lark of it, too, she decided as their high cackling old voices came to her. Said one:

"No suh, they'll never come through what we done come through."

The other old woman tuned in quaveringly:

"Lord, chile, they couldn't begin to do 't."

"Not wantin' 'im 'cause he ain't rich," chimed the first.

"Ain't none of us that, neither," vouchsafed the other.

"The ideas and the whimsies of these 'ere young'uns do beat me." They broke into high cackling laughter. The black old woman changed the basket to her other arm. The old white woman shortened the strings of her bag.

Then they were abreast of Nell. They smiled broadly upon her. The old mulatto nodded her head until the brown feather atop her brown bonnet danced like a live thing. The black old woman called out: "Howdy!"

"None of 'em will ever stand what we done stood," floated to Nell, like the refrain of a song, as she waited for the car.

Somehow the passing of those two old women changed Nell's day. For the first time, she noticed that the morning was very bright, the sky was blue and tiny knobs of green were putting out on a tree near by.

"They were so cheery, the dears!" she said of the two old women, and sought to dismiss them. She wanted to think of her own perplexities, but the old ladies insisted upon rising up before her. . . . Their cackling words: "None of 'em will ever stand what we done stood," caused Nell to toss her head defiantly. How could they know, those two. . . . Old issues that they were! Why, she herself had had her share of trouble, and she was but one of a legion of "Young'uns" as they termed them.

Had she not toiled every day except Sundays for five years, denying herself everything save sheer necessities for a chance to enjoy at some future time the heritage of every human creature, love and home and children? Undoubtedly, she had saved a little, her dowry, she called it, but its amount was written in her brain and on her heart. Tolling off their joint income, dollar by dollar, penny by penny, she and Horace together, was a part of their Sunday's routine.

Sundays, Nell often said, were Horace-days. Horace had Sundays off also, and they spent their one free day together. For the most part they spent the day planning, making schemes to make their dreams come true. While she had merely worked, Horace had slaved; he had scraped together a sum that matched her own savings and there was a little place up-state where he wished to make their home.

He wanted to marry at once, now that the little place was paid for, but then, Nell countered, when during the long years since they had known they belonged to each other, had he not wanted to do so?

As though some of the glow from the steady flame of his adoration reached out to her, Nell felt her cheeks grow hot.

Suddenly, she knew that it was hard on Horace, harder than upon herself. Black men really had tougher sledding than black women, she thought, tenderly. She loved him so, she communed in her heart. That's why she wanted things; demanded them, those things that later, would insure their peace and contentment in their nest of a home. That's why. . . . She checked herself, smiling whimsically at finding herself beginning to use all the arguments that she was wont to use upon Horace over and over to convince him that they must work on and wait a little longer.

Then for no reason at all, two old figures lumbered through her consciousness, glimmeringly like moving shadows on a wall.

One very black and stout old lady, one very stout and white old lady said: "No suh, they'll never come through what we done come through."

"Lord, chile, they couldn't begin to do 't."

Nell tossed back her head and laughed. . . . The darling funny old dears!

Aroused from her day-dreams, her slender brown fingers played for a time on the keys of her typewriter, but thoughts of Horace would not down. As the moments sped, her thoughts became laden with foreboding: she decided to call him. It was against the rules, but just this once.

—Employees must not use telephone during working-hours, except emergencies.—

A placard advised her as she dialed. It was emergency, she concluded grimly. Never before had such warning intuition driven her. Never before had a desire to call to Horace through space tormented her as it did now; never before had longing, intense as pain, made her want to stretch out her arms and encircle him, close to her heart. . . .

"Horace Canning has quit the company," an ironic voice informed her over the wire.

"Horace—quit—his—job?" Nell gasped the words foolishly and was restored to sanity only by the sound of the faint click striking into her ear.

She alighted from the car four blocks from home. She had not found Horace, though she had verified the information received by telephone. Horace had given up his job, though that no longer mattered; she had lost hers too. She had given it up to look for Horace.

She could not avoid seeing the knot of people gathered on the corner. A cursory glance revealed it to be several boys in their teens and younger mingling with the usual motley street-crowd that is attracted willy-nilly to anything that happens. Intent with her own concern she was hastening on when some horrid cataclysm rushed out to meet her, paralyzing her until sight and sound and feeling swirled and clashed into one agonizing tempest of emotion that sent her running, screaming headlong into the crowd. Horace was in the midst of it, a disheveled funny-looking Horace, but her Horace!

Magically, they made way for her to pass. . . . Save for a few taunts—a prolonged "Boo," "Sic 'em, Sic 'em," "Atta Girl," "Geese"—nothing was done to hinder her. Presently she was beside Horace, placing trembling hands upon his shoulder. At her touch, he turned, looked at her a moment, unknowingly, and announced thickly:—

"I need-sh my girl, hic, but she-sh won't-sh have me!"

Nell's grasp on his shoulder tightened; she shook him furiously. . . . "Horace, oh Horace, how could you? How could you?"

The crowd dwindled away. As for that, Nell had forgotten that there ever was a crowd. She looked for a taxi. Horace lurched heavily against her, and asked in ludicrous bewilderment:

"Is-sh you, hic, Nellie by-sh any chanc-sh?"

"Tut, tut . . ." said someone close beside her, with a voice whose high old cackle dropped through Nell's dismay like a ray of sunlight into a dark crevice.

"He be your'n, honey, your man?" queried the voice. Nell knew it belonged to the old black woman of the morning.

"Take 'im, chile, don't you dast to leave 'im, when he needs yo'," chimed in another quavering old voice.

"Just you take 'im home. A cup of right hot coffee'll fix 'im or a speck of tomatoes will be better."

Without more ado, they were walking together. The trundling gait of the two old women matching nicely with Horace's unsteady steps.

"'Tis a trouble menfolks be," offered one.

"But a sweet trouble 'tis," proffered the other.

"Trouble ain't never harmed nary one of us. What's more, us wimens can make menfolks what us choose to."

"'Deed so! Us 'tis what makes 'em or breaks 'ems."

Then they performed a tempered replica of their high cackling laughter of the morning. Soon afterwards, they left her, turning off down their street.

The next day, while Nell sat waiting proudly high-headed looking straight ahead, she was not certain that these two old ladies had really joined her. Yet without effort, she could vision the black old woman in her queer black coat and the old white woman in her brown bonnet and red-knitted sweater. Oddly enough, their high cackling old voices still rang in her ears:

"Trouble ain't never harmed nary one of us," made a tune like a Spiritual . . .

"The ideas and the whimsies of these 'ere young'uns do beat me," was an epitome of the wisdom of old age.

"No suh, they'll never come through what we done come through."

"Lord, chile, they couldn't begin to do 't," was like a skit of Negro comedy and Nell tossed back her head and laughed.

The intangibleness of those two old women enthralled her. Life, too, was like that, Nell mused, made up of intangible veils that became real only as you lifted them one by one, always, to find others and yet others, on and on. Love was one of the veils, so gossamer and fine, so fragile and easily broken. Love was one of life's veils that could never be brushed aside to grasp another. If you dared, once having it, to let it go, it was lost forever. You had to take it when you came to it, but once you caught and held it, it became for all time, a magic carpet.

Horace was coming towards her; tickets were in his hand. The porter was calling their train. Above all the ensuing bustle of departure, she caught the sound of a high, old cackle:

"'Deed so! . . . 'tis us what makes 'em or breaks 'em."

All Aboard!

At last, Horace and she were settled in their seats, on their way to the little place up-state, still short thousands of dollars of what they intended having. But she was glad, oh so glad.

"Happy?" asked Horace suddenly, his arm going around her.

"Happy!" breathed Nell with a great content.

Crisis 40 (May 1933): 109–110.

APPENDIX

First published in 1926, "Arizona and New Mexico—The Land of Esperanza" is among a series of geographical essays commissioned by editors of *Messenger*, appearing in the magazine between 1923 and 1926. Authors of essays in the series include Wallace Thurman, William Pickens, and Alice Dunbar-Nelson. The essays have since been anthologized in the 1996 collection *These "Colored" United States: African American Essays from the 1920s*, edited by Tom Lutz and Susanna Ashton.

Arizona and New Mexico—The Land of Esperanza

It is singular that most persons think of Arizona and New Mexico in unity. The fact is that Arizona was a part of New Mexico until 1863, when it was divided by Congress into a separate territory. Since each not so many years ago attained the status of Statehood, they have striven diligently, albeit amiably, to establish a distinct and separate individualism.

Yet for this once, we shall consider them as one.

Together they cover an area of 235,654 square miles, a boundless region of vast treasures.

Their mineral resources are limitless. Manganese, iron, coal, oil, zinc, copper, gold, silver, onyx and marble, meerschaum and turquoise, emeralds, sapphires, garnets and opals lie buried in level plains and rugged mountains.

Great stretches of timbered lands are protected in forest reserves, and one forest in Holebroke, Arizona, is so old, it is petrified, its trees but solid rock. The lower mountain ranges and hills are covered with stunted growth of pine, juniper, pinon, cedar, and oak. The rolling prairies are arrayed in the wonder vegetation of the Southwest—the cactus, the sagebrush, the mesquite, and the yucca.

Its surface is traversed by rivers. The greatest of these being the Rio Grande, the old reliable, of whom legend says: obligingly changed its course to suit the whim of "el Gringo"; cleaving the State of New Mexico from tip to toe as it wends its way to the Gulf. This and the Pecos and the Gila rivers along with their tributaries water extraordinarily fertile valleys; in which wonder apples, figs, apricots, grapes, wheat, corn, cotton, and alfalfa are produced. While the Colorado River in Arizona is that small and turbid stream which has wrought through centuries the mighty marvel of the Grand Canyon.

The animals and the insects of these States, like its arid vegetation, are unique. Here is the home of the Gila-monster, the vinegerone, the rattlesnake, the centipede, the tarantula and the nina de terra. The coyote and the prairie dog keep watch upon its plains, the fox and deer, the wolf and bear, sheep and mountain lions, and countless feathered "game," bestow upon their natal states the title: "The hunting ground of the United States."

Another natural resource is the climate. Rarely does the sun hide its face from these two states. Endless breezes lilt and sing as effective as an electric fan in summer and as bracing as a tonic.

Natural resources are the gifts of generous Nature, and industry is the outcome of man's manipulations of these gifts.

Since minerals are strewn in such lavish quantities, mining is an important occupation, the leading one in Arizona. Copper is yet being taken from "workings" bearing the scars and marks of the day when Spaniards conquered and enslaved the Indian, gave him the crude implements of the time and sent him chained into the bowels of the earth to delve for treasure. Later the white man came and conquered and so it is the Mexican miner rather than the Negro or the foreigner of the East who goes down and up the shaft, in and out the tunnel, down and down into endless pits in quest of minerals.

The vast stretches of grass grown plains give rise to the cattle industry, the greatest pursuit in the State of New Mexico. To all appearances and despite legend—cattle raising is an exclusive white man's trade. Mexican cowboys there are, and perhaps in a bygone day, the natives were large cattle owners—but today, one sees only the white cattleman. Occasionally one glimpses a Negro cowboy, or rather a Negro who has learned a lot about cattle; quite likely, he has often gone with cattle-trains into Kansas, Nebraska, Old Mexico to punch cattle—to prevent any of the packed cattle lying down, where they would be trodden to death beneath the hoofs of the others—on their long railway journey. But very few black men have ridden beneath the stars, singing cowboy chants to still the restless herds. And in no instance has a black American plied himself to the task of becoming one of the "big" cattlemen of the Southwest. Maybe, it is due to the side line of cattle rustling; which once upon a time accompanied cattle raising, most profitably, who knows?

In Arizona and New Mexico, man has aptly turned the climate into an industry. We have here the business of dispensing health to the health-seeker. The different chambers of commerce vie one with the other in advertisements of climate.

"Sunshine 365 days in the year," boasts New Mexico.

"Arizona—land of golden sunshine," acclaims Arizona.

Indisputably, these States offer the best in health-giving "ozone" and revivifying sun-light. The sanatorium is the outstanding feature of many towns. But Tucson, in Arizona, and Silver City, in New Mexico, are favored spots. Prescott, in Arizona, and Ft. Bayard, in New

Mexico, the latter the largest sanatorium of its kind in the country, both Veteran Bureau Hospitals, treat Negro patients. Besides these, there is no especial provision made for the Negro health-seeker. Several tentative efforts to establish a Negro sanatorium have fallen short. Yet, such an institution is a needed and certainly a humane project for an American Negro.

Again, the scenic wonders of these two States lures the tourist into their midst, while "big game" during the hunting seasons beguile the sportsmen, and so the trade of entertaining a traveling public becomes an important one.

Farming, a new and steadily growing project owing to the recently completed dams for the conservation of a bounteous water supply enabling irrigation on larger scales, the climate, the productivity of soil, and the acreage for large crops holds forth a promise of vast reward for the inhabitants of these States. Likewise, farming, more than all its other industries, swings wide its gates and cordially welcomes the Negro.

Cotton as an experiment. Cotton in the Maricopa valley and Mexican peon labor. Cotton in the Mesilla valley and Negro hands from the South. Cotton, a wonderful yield and experiment, becomes an established fact. With it all there are many Negroes in Phoenix and some scattered throughout the State. And mayhaps, Mexican peons will eventually return to Mexico. But in the Mesilla valley, Vado, a Negro town, is born. Jammed against the State's scenic highway, plodding its way to the high road of success.

As industry is dependent upon natural resources, population is dependent upon industry. It is seen, then, that industry in these States has held little promise for the Negro.

The inhabitants here are as striking as the plant and animals of Arizona and New Mexico. They are historically interesting. Consisting of fast dwindling tribes of Indians, living echoes of a by-gone day, remnants of a centuries-old civilization. The tatters of the Aztecs, cliff dwellers and the humble dwellers in Pueblos. And the Spanish-American or Mexican native, the first conquerors of Indians, plenteous whites, and essentially, it is the home of the half-breed, the inevitable outcome, where two or more races meet and mingle in an unaccustomed freedom.

While here and there are Negroes, like straggly but tenacious plants growing, nevertheless, though always in the larger towns. Becoming fewer and fewer, until in many or in all of the remoter hamlets and towns they are as sparse as rose bushes upon the prairies.

But all which the Negro has failed to give to the industry or to the population of Arizona and New Mexico, he has made amends for with the contribution to its history.

It is potent to recall that in 1538, Estevan, the Negro slave in the role of interpreter and guide to the Friar Marcos de Niza, was sent on ahead to spy upon the people and the strange lands they were entering, and send back reports to his peers. Thus, it was that Estevan the Negro was first to behold the wonders of the seven cities, and though he himself was killed, sent back the report: "Advance, the find is worth it."

Negroes have fought and struggled over all the vast stretches that included the one time Indian Territory, the Panhandle, New Mexico and Arizona, throughout the years of Indian warfare. Most of the old settlers among Negroes in "these parts" are descended or related to a hoary-haired and fast-passing, honorably discharged, Indian war fighter, who thought wearily upon receiving his discharge that "here" was as good as "way back there" to settle down and rest after his long, arduous campaign.

And mingled with the tales of Indians on warpaths are the stories of heroism performed by avenging whites and all interwoven with these deeds are mingled the deeds of solitary Negroes.

In 1916 Negroes helped patrol the borders in New Mexico and Arizona, safeguarding the doorways through which Villa or a mightier foe might enter. That Villa did enter and raided Columbus, New Mexico, was no fault of theirs. Yet they it was, who rode out in to chaparral hard on the trail of the treacherous Villa, to their death in Carrizol.

Among the famous acts of outlawry are knit the acts of black men. Oft'times they have accompanied posses in the capture of dangerous bandits. And a black man was the first to fall before the deadly aim of Billy the Kid, in a gambling hall in Silver City.

Among famous frontier huntsmen are the names of Negroes. One George Parker was the best crack shot and the gamest bear hunter who ever followed a trail. He was also a lucky prospector and amassed a fortune in mines. As did his friend John Young, who still survives; who was at one time the richest Negro and one of the wealthiest mine owners in the territory of New Mexico.

Among the lowly and humble tasks, which likewise make history, are such deeds as this: In Roswell a town of tree lined streets, it is told that a Negro, an old pioneer, recently deceased, planted the trees which grace the City's streets.

Withal, the Negroes in these States are an isolated lot, yet in nearly all instances they are home owners. In the remote hamlets, if there be blacks at all, they seem a bit hazy concerning their relationship to the great hordes of Negroes beyond their confines. This is not true of the groups in larger towns.

One is almost persuaded to say, that the brains and the brawn of the Negro population is gathered in Albuquerque. Negro enterprise of various sorts are here. Negro doctors and dentists reside here. Two churches are supported. The NAACP is represented—and it is the home of the *Southwest Review,* a Negro publication, edited by S. W. Henry.

Though the greatest outstanding feature of the Negro population is that in New Mexico, there are two exclusively Negro towns. Blackdom, sixteen miles south of Roswell and situated in the Chavis County oil area, and Vado, previously mentioned, a score of miles below Las Cruces.

So far, in New Mexico, the Negro has not yet become a bone to gnaw in politics. He is not legislated either pro or con, he is an unconsidered quantity, due to his inconsequential numbers. But what New Mexico may or may not do is evidenced in the fact that the influx of Negro children to Dona Ana County, the center of the cotton activity were not allowed to attend the schools. Separate schools were immediately installed; also Roswell in Chavis County maintains a separate school system.

On the other hand, Arizona has made rigid laws concerning her Negro inhabitants. A rather funny one is eight Negro children in any community is a sufficient quota for instituting a Negro school.

Boiled down to finality—these States are the mecca-land for the seeker after wealth—the land of every man to his own grubstake—and what-I-find-I-keep.

And criss-crossing in and out through the medley of adventure stalk the few in number black folks. Often, it is only the happy-go-lucky, black gambler; again it is but the lone and weary black prospector—but ever and ever the intrepid, stalwart Negro home-seeker forms a small yet valiant army in the land of esperanza.

And over it all the joyous freedom of the West. The unlimited re-sourcefulness, the boundless space—that either bids them stay—or baffles with its vastness—until it sends them scuttling to the North, the South, and East, whence-so-ever they have come.

For here prevails for every man be he white or black a hardier philosophy—and a bigger and better chance, that is not encountered elsewhere in these United States.

REFERENCES

Works by Anita Scott Coleman (Chronological Listing)

"Phoebe and Peter Up North." *Half-Century Magazine* 6 (Feb. 1919): 4, 10.

"Love's Power." *Half-Century Magazine* 6 (May 1919): 6.

"Phoebe Goes to a Lecture." *Half-Century Magazine* 6 (June 1919): 6.

"Billy Settles the Question." *Half-Century Magazine* 7 (Aug. 1919): 4.

"The Nettleby's New Years." *Half-Century Magazine* 8 (Jan. 1920): 5, 14–15.

"Jack Arrives." *Half-Century Magazine* 8 (Feb. 1920): 5, 14.

"El Tisico." *Crisis* 19 (March 1920): 252–253.

"'Rich Man, Poor Man—.'" *Half-Century Magazine* 8 (May 1920): 6, 14.

"Pot Luck: A Story True to Life." *Competitor* 2 (Aug.–Sept. 1920): 105–108.

"The Hand That Fed." *Competitor* 2 (Dec. 1920): 259–261, 293, 295.

"The Little Grey House." *Half-Century Magazine* 13 (July–Aug. 1922): 4, 17, 19; 13 (Sept.–Oct. 1922): 4, 21.

"Three Dogs and a Rabbit." *Crisis* 31 (January 1926): 118–122.

"The Brat." *Messenger* 8 (April 1926): 105–106, 126.

"Arizona and New Mexico—The Land of Esperanza." *Messenger* 8 (Aug. 1926): 24–25.

"Silk Stockings." *Messenger* 8 (Aug. 1926): 229–231.

"Unfinished Masterpieces." *Crisis* 34 (March 1927): 14, 24–25.

"'G'long, Old White Man's Gal . . .'" *Messenger* 10 (April 1928): 81–82.

"'White Folks's Nigger.'" *Messenger* 10 (May–June 1928): 104, 111, 114, 117, 119.

"Cross Crossings Cautiously." *Opportunity* 8 (June 1930): 177, 189.

"The Eternal Quest." *Opportunity* 9 (Aug. 1931): 242–243.

"Two Old Women A-Shopping Go! A Story of Man, Marriage and Poverty." *Crisis* 40 (May 1933): 109–110.

[Pseudonym Elizabeth Stapleton Stokes]. *Small Wisdom.* New York: Henry Harrison, 1937.

Reason for Singing. Prairie City, IL: Decker, 1948.

Singing Bells. Ill. Claudine Nankivel. Nashville: Broadman, 1961. (Children's book)

Works Consulted

Ammons, Elizabeth, comp. *Short Fiction by Black Women, 1900–1920.* New York: Oxford UP, 1991.

Anderson, Paul Allen. *Deep River: Music and Memory in Harlem Renaissance Thought.* Durham: Duke UP, 2001.

Bruck, Peter, ed. *The Black American Short Story in the 20th Century: A Collection of Critical Essays.* Amsterdam: Grüner, 1977.

Feith, Michel, ed. *Temples for Tomorrow: Looking Back at the Harlem Renaissance.* Bloomington: Indiana UP, 2001.

Gable, Craig, ed. *Ebony Rising: Short Fiction of the Greater Harlem Renaissance Era.* Bloomington: Indiana UP, 2004.

Glasrud, Bruce A., comp. *African Americans in the West: A Bibliography of Secondary Sources.* Alpine, TX: SRSU Center for Big Bend Studies, 1998.

Glasrud Bruce A., and Laurie Champion. "Anita Scott Coleman." *Twentieth Century American Women Writers, 1900–1945: A Bio-Bibliographical Critical Sourcebook.* Ed. Champion. Westport: Greenwood P, 2000. 77–81.

———, eds. *The African American West: A Century of Short Stories.* Boulder: UP of Colorado, 2000.

Hebble, Susan Morrison. "Women Writers of the Harlem Renaissance." *The History of Southern Women's Literature*. Ed. Carolyn Perry and Mary Louise Weaks. Baton Rouge: Louisiana State UP, 2002. 296–308.

Honey, Maureen, ed. *Shadowed Dreams: Women's Poetry of the Harlem Renaissance*. New Brunswick, NJ: Rutgers UP, 2006.

Huggins, Nathan Irvin. *Harlem Renaissance*. New York: Oxford UP, 1971.

Hull, Gloria T. *Color, Sex, and Poetry: Three Women Writers of the Harlem Renaissance*. Bloomington: Indiana UP, 1987.

Johnson, Abby Arthur, and Ronald Maberry Johnson. *Propaganda and Aesthetics: The Literary Politics of African-American Magazines in the Twentieth Century*. Amherst: U of Massachusetts P, 1991.

Kallenbach, Jessamine S., comp. *Index to Black American Literary Anthologies*. Boston: G. K. Hall, 1979.

Kellner, Bruce, ed. *The Harlem Renaissance: A Historical Dictionary for the Era*. New York: Methuen, 1984.

Knopf, Marcy, ed. *The Sleeper Wakes: Harlem Renaissance Stories by Women*. New Brunswick, NJ: Rutgers UP, 1993.

Lewis, David Levering. *When Harlem Was in Vogue*. New York: Oxford UP, 1979.

Lucky, Crystal J. "Black Women Writers of the Harlem Renaissance." *Challenging Boundaries: Gender and Periodization*. Ed. Joyce W. Warren and Margaret Dickie. Athens: U of Georgia P, 2000. 91–106.

Lutz, Tom, and Susanna Ashton, eds. *These "Colored" United States: African American Essays from the 1920s*. New Brunswick, NJ: Rutgers UP, 1996.

McKay, Nellie Y. Foreword. *The Sleeper Wakes: Harlem Renaissance Stories by Women*. Ed. Marcy Knopf. New Brunswick, NJ: Rutgers UP, 1993. ix–xiii.

Mullen, Bill, ed. *Revolutionary Tales: African American Women's Short Stories, from the First Story to the Present*. New York: Laurel, 1995.

Mullen, Bill. "'A Revolutionary Tale': In Search of African American Women's Short Story Writing." *American Women Short Story Writers: A Collection of Critical Essays*. Ed. Julie Brown. New York: Garland, 1995. 191–207.

Murphy, Beatrice, ed. *Negro Voices: An Anthology of Contemporary Verse*. New York: Henry Harrison, 1938.

Musser, Judith. "African American Women's Short Stories in the Harlem Renaissance: Bridging a Tradition." *Melus* 23 (1998): 27–47.

Orlando, Emily J. "'Feminine Calibans' and 'Dark Madonnas of the Grave': The Imaging of Black Women in the New Negro Renaissance." *New Voices on the Harlem Renaissance: Essays on Race, Gender, and Literary Discourse.* Ed. Australia Tarver and Paula C. Barnes. Madison, NJ: Fairleigh Dickinson UP, 2005. 59–95.

Patton, Venetria K., and Maureen Honey, eds. *Double-Take: A Revisionist Harlem Renaissance Anthology.* New Brunswick, NJ: Rutgers UP, 2001.

Roses, Lorraine Elena, and Ruth Elizabeth Randolph. "Coleman, Anita Scott." *Harlem Renaissance and Beyond: Literary Biographies of 100 Black Women Writers, 1900–1945.* Ed. Roses and Randolph. Boston: G. K. Hall, 1990. 59–62.

————, eds. *Harlem's Glory: Black Women Writing, 1900–1950.* Cambridge: Harvard UP, 1996.

————, eds. *The Harlem Renaissance and Beyond: Literary Biographies of 100 Black Women Writers, 1900–1945.* Boston: G. K. Hall, 1990.

Shockley, Ann Allen, ed. *Afro-American Women Writers, 1746–1933: An Anthology and Critical Guide.* New York: New American Library, 1988.

————. "Coleman, Anita Scott." *Afro-American Women Writers, 1746–1933: An Anthology and Critical Guide.* Ed. Shockley. New York: New American Library, 1988. 448–449.

Tarver, Australia, and Paula C. Barnes, eds. *New Voices on the Harlem Renaissance: Essays on Race, Gender, and Literary Discourse.* Madison, NJ: Fairleigh Dickinson UP, 2005.

Taylor, Quintard. *In Search of the Racial Frontier: African Americans in the American West, 1528–1990.* New York: Norton, 1998.

Vogel, Todd, ed. *The Black Press: New Literary and Historical Essays.* New Brunswick, NJ: Rutgers UP, 2001.

Wall, Cheryl A. *Women of the Harlem Renaissance.* Bloomington: Indiana UP, 1995.

Walter, John C. *The Harlem Fox: J. Raymond Jones and Tammany, 1920–1970.* New York: State U of New York P, 1988.

Wilson, Sondra Kathryn, ed. *The Crisis Reader: Stories, Poetry, and Essays from the N.A.A.C.P.'s Crisis Magazine.* New York: Modern Library, 1999.

————, ed. *The Messenger Reader: Stories, Poetry, and Essays from The Messenger Magazine.* New York: Modern Library, 2000.

————, ed. *The Opportunity Reader: Stories, Poetry, and Essays from the Urban League's Opportunity Magazine.* New York: Modern Library, 1999.

Wintz, Cary D. *Black Culture and the Harlem Renaissance.* College Station: Texas A&M UP, 1996.

————, ed. *The Harlem Renaissance: An Anthology.* Maplecrest, NY: Brandywine P, 2003.

Wintz, Cary D., and Paul Finkelman, eds. *Encyclopedia of the Harlem Renaissance.* New York: Routledge, 2004.

Witalec, Janet, ed. *Harlem Renaissance: A Gale Critical Companion.* Detroit: Gale, 2002.

Young, Mary E. "Anita Scott Coleman: A Neglected Harlem Renaissance Writer." *CLA Journal* 40 (1997): 271–287.